MACARONI

Macaroni is one of the most nutritious farinaceous foods. It is made from Italian wheat, which contains more flesh-forming matter than butcher's meat. In the manufacture of macaroni some of the bran is removed from the flour, but the meal left is still very rich in flesh-forming matter. As the coarser particles of the bran have been taken away, macaroni is slightly constipating, and must therefore always be eaten with green vegetables, onions, or fruit. Macaroni should always be boiled before being made into various dishes. It may be cooked in plain water, or in milk and water; a little salt may be added by those who use it, and care should be taken to use just enough water to cook it in, so that when the macaroni is done, little or no fluid may be left, but if any does remain it should be saved for sauce, stock for soup, &c., as it contains valuable nutritive material. Macaroni takes from 20 minutes to 1 hour to cook, according to the kind used. That which is slightly yellow is to be preferred to the white, as the latter is usually poorer than the former in mineral salts and flesh-forming substances. From 2 to 4 oz. may be regarded as the amount to be allowed at a meal for grown-up persons.

A very simple nourishing and satisfying meal can be made from macaroni plainly boiled; it may be eaten with any kind of vegetables, or baked potatoes, or fried onions, and if desired, with grated cheese, onion, caper, or parsley sauce.

MACARONI (Italian).

1/2 lb. of spaghetti or vermicelli, 2 oz. of butter, 2 eggs, 3 oz. of grated cheese, 1 tablespoonful of finely chopped parsley, pepper and salt to taste. Boil the macaroni till tender in 2 pints of water, to which the butter has been added. When soft add seasoning, the cheese, and the parsley. Beat the eggs well in the dish in which the macaroni is to be served, pour over the mixture of macaroni and other ingredients, mix all well with the eggs, and serve. If neither spaghetti nor vermicelli are handy, use Naples macaroni.

MACARONI CHEESE.

1/2 lb. of macaroni, 8 oz. of grated cheese, some breadcrumbs, pepper and salt to taste, and 1 oz. of butter. Boil the macaroni in slightly salted water until soft. Then place a layer of it in a pie-dish, sprinkle some of the grated cheese over it, dust with pepper, and repeat the layers of macaroni and cheese, finishing with a sprinkling of cheese, and the breadcrumbs. Cut the butter in pieces, and place them here and there on the top. Bake it in a moderately hot oven until brown. Eat with vegetables and tomato sauce. For those who have a weak digestion plain boiled macaroni with grated cheese added at table is better and lighter. Macaroni requires from 25 minutes to 1/2 an hour cooking. The Genoa macaroni takes longer, the thin spaghetti kind is done in from 15 to 20 minutes, and vermicelli and Italian paste are done in a few minutes. Macaroni should be thrown into boiling water and be kept boiling, as the pipes or pieces otherwise stick together. The Italian paste is mostly used as an addition in clear soup.

MACARONI CREAM.

6 oz. of macaroni, 3 oz. of cheese, 1/2 oz. of butter, 3/4 pint of milk, 1 teaspoonful of Allinson cornflour, pepper and salt to taste. Boil the macaroni until tender in only as much water as it will absorb. Make a sauce of the milk, cornflour, and cheese (you can use Parmesan, Gruyère, or Canadian cheese). Place the macaroni in a pie-dish, pour the sauce over it, grate some more cheese over the top, and let the macaroni brown in the oven.

MACARONI SAVOURY.

4 oz. of boiled macaroni, 4 oz. of Allinson fine wheatmeal, 3 eggs, 3/4 pint of milk, 1 finely chopped onion, the grated rind of 1 lemon, 2 oz. of grated cheese, 1 tablespoonful of finely chopped parsley, 1 oz. of butter, 1/2 a saltspoonful of grated nutmeg, pepper and salt to taste. Cut the macaroni in small pieces. Make a batter of the milk, eggs, and meal, mix into it all the other ingredients, pour it into a buttered pie-dish, cut up the butter in pieces and spread them on the top. Bake the savoury for 1 to 1-1/2 hours.

RICE

In many households it seems a difficulty to get rice cooked properly, that is having all the grains separate. Very often it comes to table in a soft, pulpy mass, which is certainly not appetising. To cook it in a large saucepanful of water which is then drained away is very wasteful, for a great deal of the goodness of the rice is thrown away. The following recipe will be found thoroughly reliable and satisfactory.

RICE, HOW TO COOK.

1 lb. of good rice, 1 quart of water, 1 oz. of butter, salt to taste. Wash the rice and set it over the fire with 1 quart of cold water, the butter and salt. Let it come to the boil gently, stirring it a little to prevent the rice from sticking to the saucepan. When the rice boils, set it on the side and let it just simmer. It will be sufficiently cooked in 15 to 20 minutes and each grain will be separate. Rice should not be cooked too soft, only just cooked through.

CURRIED RICE.

1 lb. of Patna rice, 1 quart of cold water, 1 dessertspoonful of curry, 1 oz. of butter, and salt to taste. Wash the rice, mix the curry with the proper quantity of water, and set the rice over the fire with it, adding the butter and seasoning. Let the rice come to the boil slowly, and stir it a few times to prevent it sticking to the saucepan. When the rice boils, cover it with a piece of buttered paper, and let it cook very gently, not stirring it again. When all the water is absorbed, serve the rice. Do not allow it to get very soft; the rice will take from 15 to 20 minutes' cooking only.

CURRIED RICE AND TOMATOES.

1/2 lb. of Patna rice, 1 dessertspoonful of curry powder, salt to taste, and 1 oz. of butter. Wash the rice; mix 1 pint of cold water with the curry powder, put this over the fire with the rice, butter, and salt. Cover the rice with a piece of buttered paper and let it simmer gently until the water is absorbed. This will take about 20 minutes. Rice cooked this way will have all the grains separate. For the tomatoes proceed as follows: 1 lb. of tomatoes and a little butter, pepper and salt. Wash the tomatoes and place them in a flat tin with a few spoonfuls of water; dust them with pepper and salt, and place little bits of butter on each tomato. Bake them from 15 to 20 minutes, according to the size of the tomatoes and the heat of the oven. Place the rice in the centre of a hot flat dish, put the tomatoes round it, pour the liquid over the rice, and serve.

PORTUGUESE RICE.

1 teacupful of rice, 3 medium-sized onions, 3 tomatoes, 2 oz. of grated cheese, 1/2 teaspoonful of herbs, 1 oz. of butter, pepper and salt to taste. Peel and slice the onions and tomatoes and fry them in the butter for 15 minutes; place the rice over the fire with 1 pint of water; add the onions, tomatoes, herbs, and seasoning, and let all cook until the rice is quite soft; serve in a vegetable dish with the grated cheese sprinkled over.

RICE AND LENTILS.

Boil the rice as above; stew Egyptian lentils with chopped onions, pepper, salt, and a little butter, until well done. Put the rice on a dish, pour over the stewed onions and lentils, serve, and eat with green vegetables.

RICE AND ONIONS.

Boil whole onions in water until done quite through, remove them from the water, and put in it washed rice with a little pepper, salt, and butter. When done, serve with the onions and eat with a green vegetable.

SAVOURY RICE (Italian).

1 breakfastcupful of rice, 4 tablespoonfuls of grated cheese (Parmesan or other cheese), 1 oz. of butter, a pinch of saffron, pepper and salt to taste. Boil the rice with water as above, then add the cheese, butter, saffron, and seasoning; mix all well, and serve.

SAVOURY RICE CROQUETTES.

1/2 lb. of Patna rice, 1-1/2 pints of milk, 1 lb. of Spanish onions, 1 oz. of butter, 2 eggs, 1 teacupful of raspings, Allinson's oil for frying. Boil the rice in the milk until soft, and turn it out to get quite cold. Meanwhile chop the onions up fine and fry them brown in the butter. Form the cold rice into balls, and with the thumb of the right hand hollow them sufficiently to admit of their receiving a stuffing of fried onions, close them again carefully, dip them in the eggs beaten up and then in the raspings, and fry them in boiling oil a light brown. Serve with gravy. There are various stuffings which can be used instead of the onions—fried mushrooms chopped up, some olives chopped fine and mixed with hard-boiled yolks of eggs, &c.

SPANISH RICE.

6 onions, 6 tomatoes, 1-1/2 pints of vegetable stock, herbs and seasoning, 1-1/2 cupfuls of rice, butter. Fry the onions and tomatoes in butter until well

browned, then place them with the seasoning into the cold stock, and add the rice. When all have boiled slowly for 20 minutes, the rice should have absorbed the stock. Serve with cheese grated over.

OMELETS

CHEESE OMELET.

4 slices of Allinson bread toasted, or Allinson rusks, 3 eggs, 1/4 lb. of grated cheese, 1 saltspoonful of nutmeg, 1 pint of milk, 2 oz. of butter, pepper and salt to taste. Beat up the eggs, and mix them with the milk; crush the toast or rusks with your hands, and soak them in the egg and milk. Add the cheese, nutmeg, and seasoning. Dissolve half of the butter and mix it with the other ingredients. Butter a pie-dish, pour in the mixture, cut the rest of the butter in little pieces, and scatter them over the top. Bake the savoury for 1 hour or a little longer until well set. Serve hot or cold.

FRENCH BEAN OMELET.

3 tablespoonfuls of cut boiled French beans, 4 eggs, 1 dessertspoonful of Allinson fine wheatmeal, 1/2 a teacupful of milk, 2 tablespoonfuls of grated cheese (Gruyère or Parmesan), pepper and salt to taste, some vege-butter or oil for frying. Smooth the meal with the milk, beat up the eggs and add them, the cheese and seasoning to the meal and milk; mix thoroughly with the beans, and fry the omelet in boiling butter or Allinson frying oil.

FRENCH OMELET WITH CHEESE.

3 eggs, 1 oz. of grated cheese, 3 dessertspoonfuls of water, pepper and salt to taste, and 1 oz. of butter. Beat the yolks of the eggs, add to them the water and seasoning; whip the whites of the eggs to a stiff froth, and mix it lightly with the yolks. Meanwhile have the butter boiling hot in an omelet

pan, pour the mixture into it, and let it fry over a gentle fire. Pass a heated salamander or coal-shovel over the top of the omelet. When it has risen, scatter the cheese over it; let the omelet cook a little longer, fold over when the top is still creamy, and serve immediately.

GARDENER'S OMELET.

1 breakfastcupful of cold boiled vegetables, minced fine (green peas, carrots, turnips, potatoes, &c.), 4 eggs, 1 tablespoonful of Allinson fine wheatmeal, 1/2 a gill of milk, pepper and salt, and a little nutmeg to taste, 1 oz. of butter. Beat the eggs and milk well together, rub the meal smooth with it, add the vegetables and seasoning, and fry as an omelet. Serve with sauce.

OMELET HERB.

4 slices of Allinson bread, 1 pint of milk, 1 finely chopped English onion, 1 good tablespoonful of finely chopped parsley, 1 teaspoonful of dried mixed herbs, 3 eggs, 2 oz. of butter, pepper and salt to taste. Soak the bread, fry the onion in 1-1/2 oz. of butter, and mix it with the soaked bread. Add the herbs, parsley, and seasoning, and mix all well. Butter a pie-dish with the rest of the butter, pour the mixture into it, and bake.

OMELET LENTIL.

It you have any cold boiled lentils, for instance, some sandwich mixture you wish to use up, proceed as follows: To 1 teacupful of boiled lentils take 3 well-beaten eggs, and pepper and salt to taste. Add 1 dessertspoonful of water to each egg, and mix the lentils and eggs smooth. Fry the mixture as an omelet in boiling butter.

OMELET MACARONI.

3 oz. of boiled cold macaroni, 3 eggs, 1 dessertspoonful of finely chopped parsley, 1-1/2 oz. of grated cheese, 1/2 a saltspoonful of nutmeg, pepper and salt to taste, 1-1/2 oz. of butter. Cut the macaroni into little pieces; beat the eggs well, and mix them with the macaroni. Add the seasoning, parsley, cheese, and nutmeg; mix all well, and fry the omelet with the butter in a large frying-pan.

OMELET ONION.

4 medium-sized English onions, 1-1/2 oz. of butter, 2 oz. of Allinson breadcrumbs, 4 eggs, 4 tablespoonfuls of milk, pepper and salt to taste. Peel and slice the onions, bake them in a pie-dish with the butter and seasoning, until quite soft. Whip the eggs up, mix them with the milk, breadcrumbs, and the baked onions. Put the mixture into a greased pie-dish, and bake in a moderately hot oven. Serve with tomato sauce.

OMELET SAVOURY.

Soak Allinson wholemeal bread in cold milk and water until soft, then rub smooth, grate 1 onion, beat up 1 egg, and add a few flavouring herbs, and pepper and salt to taste. Mix the whole together, put in a pie-dish, place a few small pieces of butter on the top, and bake about 1/2 hour, or until done. Eat with vegetables and potatoes.

OMELET SOUFFLÉ.

4 eggs, 3 oz. of sifted castor sugar, the grated rind of 1/2 a lemon, 1 oz. of butter. Beat the yolks of the eggs for 10 minutes with the sugar and lemon rind. Whip the whites of the eggs to a very stiff froth, mix it with the other ingredients, pour the mixture into a well-buttered pie-dish or cake tin, and

bake the Soufflé in a moderately hot oven from 10 to 15 minutes. Serve immediately.

OMELET SOUFFLÉ (SWEET).

6 eggs, 3 oz. of powdered sugar, 1 oz. of butter, 1 dessertspoonful of potato flour, and 1 dessertspoonful of orangeflower water. Put the yolks of the eggs into a large basin, add the sugar, potato flour, and orange water, and beat all well with a wooden spoon for 10 minutes; beat the whites of the eggs to a stiff froth, and mix them lightly with the other ingredients. Meanwhile beat the butter in the omelet pan; when boiling pour the mixture into it, and fry the omelet over a gentle fire. When it begins to set round the sides shake it very gently from side to side, and turn the omelet neatly out on a buttered dish. Set it in the oven for about 10 minutes, and serve immediately with a little castor sugar sifted over it.

OMELET TOMATO (1).

This is made in almost the same way as the savoury omelet, but without the addition of flavouring herbs. 2 average-sized tomatoes are cut up fine, and mixed with the ingredients given above. When tinned tomatoes are used the juice may be made hot and the bread soaked in it instead of in milk and water.

OMELET TOMATO (2).

1 lb. of tomatoes, 1/2 lb. of breadcrumbs, 1 large Spanish onion, 3 eggs, 2 oz. of butter, pepper and salt to taste. Stew the finely chopped onions in the butter for 20 minutes in a covered-up saucepan, add pepper and salt, cut the tomatoes up, add these to the other ingredients. Let all simmer for 20 minutes; pour the mixture over the breadcrumbs, add the eggs well beaten,

mix all up thoroughly, and turn the mixture into one or more well-buttered shallow tins. Bake the omelet in a quick oven for 10 to 15 minutes.

OMELET TRAPPIST.

4 oz. of fine breadcrumbs, 2 eggs, 1-1/2 oz. of butter, 1/2 teaspoonful of powdered herbs, pepper and salt to taste, 1/2 gill of boiling milk. Moisten the breadcrumbs with the milk, add the eggs well beaten, the herbs and seasoning. Mix all well and smoothly. Melt the butter in the frying-pan, spread the mixture in it, and fry the omelet a golden brown both sides.

SWEET OMELET (1).

3 eggs, 2 oz. of butter, sugar to taste, 1 lemon, and 1/2 a teacupful of new milk. Whip the yolks of the eggs well, adding the grated rind of the lemon, half the butter melted, the milk, and sugar. Just before frying the omelet, add the lemon juice and the whites of the eggs whipped to a stiff froth. Make the rest of the butter boiling hot in an oval omelet pan, the size of the dish on which it is to be served, and fry till lightly browned. Sift sugar over it, and serve immediately.

SWEET OMELET (2).

1/2 pint of new milk, 4 eggs, cinnamon and sugar to taste, 1 oz. of butter, and 1 teaspoonful of Allinson fine wheatmeal. Smooth the wheatmeal with the milk, and mix with the other ingredients. Make the butter boiling hot in a frying-pan, and fry the omelet till lightly browned. Serve immediately with sugar sifted over it.

SWEET OMELET (3).

5 eggs, 1 tablespoonful of castor sugar, 2 tablespoonfuls of water, 2 oz. of butter, some raspberry and currant jam. Melt the butter in an omelet pan, beat the eggs well, stir in the sugar, and pour the mixture into the hot butter. Fry a pale golden colour, and turn it on to a hot dish. Spread some jam on the omelet, double it, and serve at once. The inside of the omelet should remain creamy.

VEGETABLES

GREEN VEGETABLES (General Remarks).

I have not given recipes for the cooking of plain greens, as they are prepared very much alike everywhere in England. There are a number of recipes in this book giving savoury ways of preparing them, and I will now make a few remarks on the cooking of plain vegetables. The English way of boiling them is not at all a good one, as most of the soluble vegetable salts, which are so important to our system, are lost through it. Green vegetables are generally boiled in a great deal of salt water; this is drained off when they are tender, and the vegetables then served. A much better way for all vegetables is to cook them in a very small quantity of water, and adding a small piece of butter (1 oz. to 2 lb. of greens) and a little salt. When the greens are tender, any water which is not absorbed should be thickened with a little Allinson fine wheatmeal and eaten with the vegetables. A great number of them, such as *Cabbages, Savoys, Brussel sprouts, Scotch kail, turnip-tops, &c., &c.*, can be prepared this way.

In the case of vegetables like *asparagus, cauliflower, sea kale, parsnips, artichokes, carrots* or *celery*, which cannot always be stewed in a little water, this should be saved as stock for soups or sauces. Most of these vegetables are very nice with a white sauce; carrots are particularly pleasant with parsley sauce.

Spinach is a vegetable which English cooks rarely prepare nicely; the Continental way of preparing it is as follows: The spinach is cooked without water, with a little salt; when quite tender it is strained, turned on to a board, and chopped very finely; then it is returned to the saucepan with a piece of butter, a little nutmeg, or a few very finely chopped eschalots and some of the juice previously strained. When the spinach is cooking a little Allinson fine wheatmeal, smoothed in 1 or 2 tablespoonfuls of milk, is added to bind the spinach with the juice; cook it a few minutes longer, and serve it with slices of hard-boiled egg on the top. *Potatoes* also require a good deal of care. When peeled, potatoes are plainly boiled, they should be placed over the fire after the water has been strained; the potatoes should be lightly shaken to allow the moisture to steam out. This makes them mealy and more palatable. Potatoes which have been baked in their skins should be pricked when tender, or the skins be cracked in some way, otherwise they very soon become sodden. A very palatable way of serving potatoes, is to peel them and bake them in a tin with a little oil or butter, or vege-butter; they should be turned occasionally, in order that they should brown evenly. This is not a very hygienic way of preparing potatoes. From a health point of view they are best baked in their skins, or steamed with or without the skins. A good many vegetables may be steamed with advantage; for instance, *cabbage, sprouts, turnips, parsnips, swedes, Scotch kail, &c.* Any way of preparing greens is better than boiling them in a large saucepanful of water and throwing this away. I may just mention that Scotch kail, after being boiled in a little water, should be treated exactly as spinach, and is most delicious in that way; an onion cooked with it greatly improves the flavour.

ARTICHOKES À LA SAUCE BLANCHE.

2 lbs. of artichokes, 1 oz. of Allinson fine wheatmeal, 3/4 pint of milk, 1 egg, juice of 1/2 a lemon, pepper and salt to taste. Peel the artichokes, and boil them in water until tender; cut them into slices 1/2 an inch thick and place them on a dish. Make a sauce of the milk and meal with seasoning; when the sauce has thickened, remove it from the fire, beat up the egg with the lemon juice and add both to the sauce, pour it over the artichokes, and serve.

ARTICHOKES À LA PARMESAN.

2 lbs. of artichokes, 3/4 pint of milk, 1 tablespoonful of Allinson fine wheatmeal, 1 egg, juice of 1/2 a lemon, 2 oz. of grated Parmesan or any

other cooking cheese. Proceed as in the recipe for "Celery à la Parmesan," add the cheese to the sauce, and serve the same with sauce as above.

ASPARAGUS (BOILED).

Scrape the white parts of the stalks quite clean, and put them into cold water as they are done. Tie them up into bundles, and cut them all the same length. Now put them into a saucepan, cover with boiling water, add a little salt, and boil gently and steadily for 20 to 30 minutes. Take them out of the water as soon as they are tender, and dish on to rounds of toast with the points to the middle. Serve with them rich melted butter in a tureen.

CABBAGE.

Remove the outer coarse leaves, cut the cabbage in four pieces lengthways, and well wash the pieces in salt water. The salt is added because it kills any insects which may be present. Wash the cabbage as often as is necessary in pure water after this to clean it and remove the salt, and then shred it up fine. Set it over the fire with 1/2 pint of water, 1 oz. of butter, a dash of pepper, and a very little salt. Let it cook very gently for 2 hours; when it is quite tender, the liquid can be thickened with a little fine wheatmeal; smooth this with a little milk, or water if milk is not handy; boil it up, and serve.

CARROTS WITH PARSLEY SAUCE.

Scrub and wash as many carrots as are required. Cook them in a little water or steam them until quite tender, then slice them and place them in a saucepan. Make a white sauce as directed in the recipe for "Onions and white sauce," and stir into it a handful of finely-chopped parsley. Pour the sauce over the carrots, and let them simmer for ten minutes. Serve very hot with baked potatoes.

CAULIFLOWER WITH WHITE SAUCE.

Trim the cauliflower, cutting away only the bad and bruised leaves and the coarse part of the stalk. Put it into salt water to force out any insects in the cauliflower. After soaking, wash it well in fresh water and boil quickly until tender, and serve with white sauce.

CELERY (ITALIAN).

2 heads of celery, 1/2 pint of milk, 1 oz. of butter, 1 egg, 1 cupful of breadcrumbs, pepper and salt to taste. Cut up the celery into pieces, boil it in water for 10 minutes; drain it and put it into the stewpan with the milk, 1/2 oz. butter, pepper and salt. Simmer the celery gently until tender, put it aside to cool a little, and add the egg well beaten. Butter a shallow dish, strew it well with some of the breadcrumbs, and pour in the celery, sprinkle the rest of the breadcrumbs over the top, put the butter over it in little bits, and bake the celery until brown.

CELERY (STEAMED) WITH WHITE CHEESE SAUCE.

Prepare the celery as in previous recipe, leaving it in long pieces, and place it in a vegetable steamer, which consists of a large saucepan over which is fitted a perforated top. Add a little pepper and salt, and let the celery steam for 1-1/2 hours. For the sauce you need: 1 pint of milk, 1 oz. of butter, 1 dessertspoonful of Allinson cornflour, 1-1/2 oz. of grated cheese, pepper and salt to taste. Boil the milk with the butter, thicken it with the cornflour smoothed first with a spoonful of water, and last add the grated cheese and seasoning; let the sauce simmer, stirring it until the cheese is dissolved.

Have ready some Allinson plain rusks on a flat dish, place the celery on it, pour the sauce over, and serve very hot.

CELERY (STEWED) WITH WHITE SAUCE.

2 or 3 heads of celery (according to quantity required), 2 oz. of butter, 1 dessertspoonful of flour, 1/2 pint of milk, pepper and salt to taste. Remove the outer hard pieces from the celery, saving them for flavouring soups or sauces; wash well and cut up in pieces about 3 inches long. Set over the fire with 1/2 pint of water, the butter and seasoning. Let cook gently until the celery is quite tender, which will take about 1 hour; add the thickening and the milk. Let all gently simmer for a few minutes, and serve.

LEEKS.

Remove the coarse part of the green stalks of the leeks. If the leeks are gritty cut them right through and wash them well, and if necessary use a brush to get out the sand. Tie the leeks in bunches and steam them until tender, which will take about 1-1/2 hours. Make a white sauce as for the cauliflower. Put the leeks on pieces of dry toast on a flat dish, pour the sauce over them, and serve.

MUSHROOMS (STEWED).

1 lb. of mushrooms, 1 oz. of butter, 1/2 pint of water, 1/2 teaspoonful of herbs, 1/2 saltspoonful of nutmeg, pepper and salt to taste, juice of 1/2 a lemon, the yolk of 1 egg, 1 dessertspoonful of Allinson cornflour. Peel and clean the mushrooms, and wash them in water with a dash of vinegar in it. Wipe them dry with a cloth; have the water and butter ready in a saucepan with the herbs, and seasoning. Stew the mushrooms in this for 10 to 15

minutes. Thicken with the cornflour, then stir in the yolk of egg with the lemon juice, and serve.

ONION TORTILLA.

1 lb. of Spanish onions, 1-1/2 oz. of butter or oil, 3 eggs. Melt the butter in a frying-pan, slice the onions, and fry them for 10 or 15 minutes, beat the eggs, add them to the onions, season with pepper and salt, and fry the whole a light brown on both sides.

ONIONS (BRAISED).

2 lbs. of onions, 2 oz. of butter, vege-butter, or oil, pepper and salt to taste. Peel and slice the onions, and fry them a nice brown in the butter. Then add enough water to make gravy, add pepper and salt, and stew the onions for 20 minutes. Eat with wholemeal toast. This is very savoury, and is much liked.

ONIONS (SPANISH) (BAKED).

Peel as many onions as are required, making an incision crossways on the top, and put in a baking-dish with 1/2 oz. of butter on each large onion, or half that quantity on small ones; dust them over with pepper and salt, and bake them for 3 hours. Keep them covered for 2 hours, and let them brown after that. Baste the onions from time to time with the butter.

SCOTCH OR CURLY KAIL.

Scotch kail is best after there has been frost on it. Wash the kail, and cut away the coarse stalks, boil it for 1-1/2 to 2 hours in a small quantity of water, adding a chopped up onion. Drain it when soft and chop it fine like spinach. Into the saucepan in which the kail was cooked put a piece of butter; melt it, and stir into it 1 tablespoonful of Allinson fine wheatmeal, and brown it very slightly. Then add some of the drained-off kail wafer and stir it smooth with the browned flour. Return the chopped Scotch kail to the saucepan, add pepper and salt to taste; let it cook for a minute, and serve.

SPINACH.

Wash the spinach thoroughly, and set it over the fire in a saucepan without any water, as enough water will boil out of the spinach to cook it. Heat it gently at first, stirring it a few times to prevent it burning, until enough water has boiled out of the spinach to prevent it from catching. Let the spinach cook 20 minutes, then strain it through a colander, pressing the water out with a wooden spoon or plate. Put a piece of butter in the saucepan in which the spinach was cooked; when melted, stir into it a spoonful of Allinson fine wheatmeal, and keep stirring the meal and butter for 1 minute over the fire. Return the spinach to the saucepan, mix it well with the butter and meal, and add as much of the strained-off water as is necessary to moisten it; add pepper and salt to taste, and a little lemon juice. Let the spinach heat well through before serving. Have ready 1 or 2 hard-boiled eggs cut in slices, and decorate the spinach with them. Use 1 oz. of butter, an even tablespoonful of the meal, and the juice of 1/2 a lemon to 4 lbs. of spinach.

TURNIPS (MASHED).

Peel and wash the turnips, and steam them until tender. Mash them up in a saucepan over the fire, mixing with them 1 oz. of butter. Pile the mashed turnips on a flat dish, and pour a white sauce over them.

EGG COOKERY.

Eggs are a boon to cooks, especially when dishes are wanted quickly. They enter into a great many savoury and sweet dishes, and few cakes are made without them. They can be prepared in a great variety of ways. Eggs are a good food when taken in moderation. As they are a highly nutritious article of food, they should not be indulged in too freely. Eggs contain both muscle and bone-forming material, in fact everything required for building up the organism of the young bird. The chemical composition of hen's and duck's eggs are as follows:—

```
                Hen's egg.  Duck's egg.
Water ........    74.22       71.11
Nitrogen .....    12.55       12.24
Fat ..........    12.11       15.49
Mineral matter     1.12        1.16
                 ------      ------
                 100.00      100.00
                 ======      ======
```

Eggs take a long time to digest if hard boiled. All the fat of the egg is contained in the yolk, but the white of the egg is pure albumen (or nitrogen) and water. Eggs are most easily digested raw or very lightly boiled, and best cooked thus for invalids. The best way of lightly boiling an egg is to put it in boiling water, set the basin or saucepan on the side of the stove, and let it stand just off the boil for five or six minutes. Eggs often crack when they are put into enough boiling water to well cover them, owing to the sudden expansion of the contents. If they are not covered with water there is less danger of them cracking. One can easily tell stale eggs from fresh ones by holding them up to a strong light. A fresh egg looks clear and transparent, whilst stale ones look cloudy and opaque. There are various ways of preserving eggs for the winter; one of the best is by using the Allinson egg preservative. Another very good way is to have stands made with holes which will hold the eggs. Keep these stands in an airy place in a good current of fresh air, and every week turn the eggs, so that one week they stand the pointed end down, next week the rounded end down.

APPLE SOUFFLÉ.

4 eggs, 4 apples, 2 oz. of castor sugar (or more if the apples are very sour), 1 gill of new milk or half milk and half cream, 1 oz. of Allinson cornflour, and the juice of 1 lemon. Pare, cut up, and stew the apples with the sugar and lemon juice until they are reduced to a pulp. Beat them quite smooth, and return them to the stewpan. Smooth the cornflour with the milk, and mix it with the apples, and stir until it boils; then turn the mixture into a basin to cool. Separate the yolks from the whites of the eggs; beat the yolks well, and mix them with the apple mixture. Whisk the whites to a stiff froth, mix them lightly with the rest, and pour the whole into a buttered Soufflé tin. Bake for 20 minutes in a moderately hot oven, and serve at once.

CHEESE SOUFFLÉ.

8 oz. of Parmesan or other good dry, cooking cheese, 4 eggs, 1 oz. of Allinson fine wheatmeal, 1 gill of milk, 1 oz. of butter, mustard, pepper, and salt to taste. Melt the butter in a saucepan, stir in the wheatmeal, season with mustard, pepper, and salt. Pour in the milk, and stir until the mixture is set and comes away from the sides of the saucepan. Turn into a basin, and let the mixture cool. Grate the cheese and stir it in; separate the yolks of the eggs from the whites, and drop the yolks of the eggs, one by one, into the mixture, beating all well. Whip the whites of the eggs to a stiff froth, mix it lightly with the other ingredients; turn the mixture into a buttered Soufflé tin, and bake the Soufflé for 15 minutes.

CHOCOLATE SOUFFLÉ.

5 eggs, 2 oz. of butter, 3 oz. of castor sugar, 2 large bars of chocolate, 6 oz. of the crumb of the bread, and vanilla essence to taste. Cream the butter, and stir into it gradually the yolks of the eggs, the sugar, and chocolate.

Previously soak the bread in milk or water. Squeeze it dry, and add to it the other ingredients. Add vanilla and the whites of the eggs whipped to a stiff froth, and pour the mixture into a buttered pie-dish or cake tin. Bake 3/4 of an hour, and serve immediately. If the Soufflé is baked in a cake tin, a serviette should be pinned round it before serving.

CURRIED EGGS.

6 hard-boiled eggs, 1 medium-sized English onion, 1 cooking apple, 1 teaspoonful of curry powder, 1 dessertspoonful of Allinson fine wheatmeal, 1 oz. of butter, and salt to taste. Prepare the onion and apple, chop them very fine, and fry them in the butter in a stewpan until brown. Add 1/2 pint of water and a little salt. Smooth the curry and wheatmeal with a little cold water, and thicken the sauce with it. Let it simmer for 10 minutes, then rub through a sieve. Return the sauce to the stewpan, shell the eggs, and heat them up in the sauce; serve very hot on a flat dish.

EGG AND CHEESE.

6 eggs, 1 teacupful of milk, thickened with 1 dessertspoonful of Allinson fine wheatmeal, 2 oz. of grated cheese, pepper and salt to taste. Butter a pie-dish, pour into it the thickened milk, break the eggs over it, sprinkle the cheese over them, and season to taste. Bake in a moderate oven until the eggs are just set.

EGG AND CHEESE FONDU.

To each egg 1/2 its weight in grated cheese and a 1/2 oz. of butter (if only 1 egg is prepared 1/2 oz. of butter must be used); mustard, pepper, and salt to taste. Whip up the eggs, add 1 dessertspoonful of water for each egg, as in the previous recipe; mix in the cheese, a little made mustard, and pepper and salt. Heat the butter in a frying-pan or small stewpan. When hot stir in the mixture of egg and cheese. Keep stirring it with a knife, until it becomes a smooth and thickish mass. Put on hot buttered toast, and serve. This is an extremely tasty French dish. The mixture, when cold, is excellent for sandwiches.

EGG AND TOMATO SAUCE.

4 eggs, 1 teacupful of tomato sauce, and 1/2 oz. of butter. Melt the butter in a flat dish; break the eggs carefully into it without breaking the yolks, and place the dish on the stove until the eggs are set. Heat the tomato sauce, which should be well seasoned, and pour it over the eggs. Serve very hot, with sippets of Allinson wholemeal toast.

EGG AND TOMATO SANDWICHES.

4 eggs, 1 teacupful of tinned tomatoes or 1/2 lb. fresh ones, pepper and salt, 1 oz. of butter. Melt the butter in a frying-pan, and cook the tomatoes in it until most of the liquid is steamed away; set aside to cool. If fresh tomatoes are used, they should be scalded and skinned before cooking. Beat up the eggs and stir them into the cooled tomatoes, adding seasoning to taste. Stir the eggs and tomatoes with a knife until set, then turn the mixture into a bowl to get cold, and use for sandwiches.

EGG SALAD WITH MAYONNAISE.

1 lb. of cold boiled potatoes, 6 hard-boiled eggs, the juice of 1/2 a lemon, pepper and salt to taste. Cut the potatoes and eggs into slices, dust them with pepper and salt, add the lemon juice, and mix all well together. Make the mayonnaise as follows; 1-1/2 gills of good salad oil, the yolks of 2 eggs, 1 saltspoonful of mustard, lemon juice, pepper, and salt to taste. Take a

clean cold basin, and place in it the yolks of the eggs beaten up. Drop the oil into them, drop by drop, stirring with a wooden spoon quickly all the time. Great care should be taken, especially in the beginning, as the eggs easily curdle when the oil is stirred in too fast. When the mayonnaise gets very thick add carefully a little lemon juice to thin it down, then add again oil and lemon juice alternately until all the oil is used up. Smooth the mustard with a little lemon juice, and stir it in last of all with sufficient pepper and salt. Taste the mayonnaise, and add lemon juice or seasoning as required. Vinegar may be used instead of lemon juice if the latter is not conveniently had. The mayonnaise should be made in a cold room, as it may curdle if made in a hot room. Should an accident happen, beat up another yolk of egg and start afresh with a little fresh oil, and when going on well stir in, drop by drop, the curdled mayonnaise. Mix part of it with the eggs and potatoes, and pour the rest over the salad; garnish with watercress.

EGG SALMAGUNDI WITH JAM.

4 eggs, 1 oz. of butter, the juice of 1/2 a lemon, 1/2 a teacupful of cream or milk, some apricot or other jam. Melt the butter in a frying-pan. Beat the eggs, and mix with them the cream or milk and the lemon juice. Pour the mixture into the butter, and stir it over the fire until it thickens. Stir in some jam, and serve with lady fingers, Allinson rusks, or bread fried in butter.

EGG SAVOURY.

6 hard-boiled eggs, shelled and sliced; in summer use 1 large breakfastcupful of boiled and chopped spinach; in winter Scotch kale prepared the same way; some very thin slices of bread and butter, nutmeg, pepper, and salt to taste, 1/2 pint of milk, and some butter. Butter a pie-dish and line it with slices of bread and butter. Spread a layer of spinach and a layer of slices of eggs; dust with nutmeg, pepper, and salt. Repeat the

layers, and finish with a layer of bread well buttered. Pour over the whole the milk, and bake the savoury from 20 to 30 minutes, or until brown.

EGGS À LA BONNE FEMME.

4 eggs, 1 Spanish onion, 1 oz. of butter, 1 teaspoonful of vinegar, and 2 tablespoonfuls of breadcrumbs; pepper and salt to taste. Peel and slice the onion, and fry it brown in the butter; add the vinegar and seasoning when done. Spread the onion on a buttered dish, break the eggs over them, dust these with pepper and salt, and sprinkle with breadcrumbs. Place a few bits of butter on the top, and bake until the eggs are set, which will only take a few minutes.

EGGS À LA DUCHESSE.

1 quart of milk, 6 eggs, 1 tablespoonful of Allinson cornflour, sugar to taste, a piece of vanilla 2 inches long. Splice the vanilla and let it boil with the milk and sugar; smooth the cornflour with a spoonful of water, thicken the milk with it, and let it cook gently for 2 or 3 minutes; remove the vanilla. Have ready the whites of eggs whipped to a stiff froth, drop it in spoonfuls in the boiling milk; let it simmer for a few minutes until the egg snow has got set, remove the snowballs with a slice, and place them in a glass dish. Let the milk cool a little; beat up the yolks of the eggs, mix them carefully with the milk, taking care not to curdle them; stir the whole over the fire to let the eggs thicken, but do not allow it to boil. Let the mixture cool, pour the custard into the glass dish, but not pouring it over the snow; serve when quite cold. Half the quantity will make a fair dishful.

EGGS AND CABBAGE.

1 large breakfastcupful of cold boiled cabbage, 3 eggs, 1 teacupful of milk, pepper and salt to taste, 1/2 oz. of butter. Warm the cabbage with the butter and the milk; meanwhile beat up the eggs. Mix all together and season with pepper and salt. Turn the mixture into a shallow buttered pie-dish, and bake for 20 minutes. Any kind of cold vegetables mashed up can be used up this way, and will make a nice side dish for dinner.

EGGS AU GRATIN.

3 hard-boiled eggs, 1-1/2 oz. of grated cheese, 1 oz. of butter, 2 tablespoonfuls of breadcrumbs, a little nutmeg, and pepper and salt to taste. Slice the eggs, place them on a well-buttered flat baking dish, sprinkle them thickly with the grated cheese, and dust with nutmeg, pepper, and salt. Spread the breadcrumbs over the top, and scatter the butter in bits over the breadcrumbs. Bake until the breadcrumbs begin to brown.

FORCEMEAT EGGS.

6 eggs, 1 small English onion, a few leaves of fresh sage, or 1/2 teaspoonful of dried powdered sage, a few sprigs of Parsley, pepper and salt to taste, and some paste rolled thin, made of 6 oz. of Allinson fine wheatmeal, 2 oz. of butter or vege-butter, and a little cold water. Boil the eggs for 10 minutes, set them in cold water, and take off the shells. Cut them in half lengthways, remove the yolks, and proceed as follows: Chop up the onion very fine with the sage and parsley, and season with pepper and salt. Pound the yolks very fine, and add the onion and herbs; fill the whites of the eggs with the mixture. Put the halves together, enclose them in paste, brush them over with the white of egg, and bake until the pastry is done, which will take about 15 minutes. Serve with vegetables and sauce.

FRENCH EGGS.

6 hard-boiled eggs, 1/2 pint of milk, 1 oz. of butter, 1 dessertspoonful of Allinson fine wheatmeal, 1 dessertspoonful of finely chopped parsley, nutmeg, pepper, and salt to taste. Boil the milk with the butter, thicken it with the flour, smoothed previously with a little cold milk; season to taste. When the milk is thickened shell the eggs, cut them into quarters lengthways, and put them into the sauce. Last of all, put in the parsley, and serve with sippets of toast laid in the bottom of the dish.

MUSHROOM AND EGGS.

4 hard-boiled eggs, 1/4 lb. of mushrooms, 1 teaspoonful of parsley chopped very fine, 1 oz. of butter, pepper and salt. Stew the mushrooms in the butter, and season well; chop up the eggs and mix them with the mushrooms, adding the parsley; heat all well through, and serve on sippets of toast.

MUSHROOM SOUFFLÉ.

4 eggs, 1 oz. of Allinson fine wheatmeal, 1 oz. of butter, 6 oz. of mushrooms, pepper and salt to taste. Peel, wash, and cut in small pieces the mushrooms, and stew them in 3/4 of a teacupful of water. When the mushrooms have stewed 10 minutes, drain off the liquid, which should be a teacupful. Melt the butter in a little saucepan, stir into it the wheatmeal, and when this is well mixed with the butter, add the mushroom liquor, stirring the mixture well until quite smooth and thick and coming away from the sides of the saucepan. Then stir in the mushrooms, and turn all into a basin and let it cool a little. Separate the yolks from the whites of the eggs, and stir each yolk separately into the mixture in the basin. Season to taste. Whip up the whites of the eggs to a stiff froth, and mix them lightly with the rest. Turn the mixture into a buttered pie-dish or Soufflé tin, and bake the Soufflé 15 minutes.

POACHED EGGS.

Unless an egg-poacher is used, eggs are best poached in a large frying-pan nearly filled with water. A little vinegar and salt should be added to the water, as the eggs will then set more quickly. Each egg should first be broken into a separate cup, and then slipped into the rapidly boiling water; cover them up and allow them to boil only just long enough to have the whites set, which will take about 2 minutes. Quite newly laid eggs take a little longer. Have ready hot buttered toast, remove the eggs from the water with an egg-slice, and slip them on the toast. Always have plates and dishes very hot for all kinds of egg dishes. Poached eggs are also a very nice accompaniment to vegetables, like spinach, Scotch kale, &c., when they are served laid on the vegetables.

POTATO SOUFFLÉ.

2 oz. of butter, 4 eggs, 1/4 lb. of castor sugar, 1/2 oz. of ground almonds (half bitter and half sweet), 6 oz. of cold boiled and grated potatoes, and 1-1/2 oz. of sifted breadcrumbs. Cream the butter in a basin, which is done by stirring it round the sides of the basin until soft and creamy, when it will make a slight crackling noise. Stir in the yolks of the eggs, the sugar, and almonds; beat for 10 minutes, then stir in the potatoes and breadcrumbs, and last of all the whites of the eggs whipped to a stiff froth. Turn the mixture into a well-buttered dish, and bake in a moderately hot oven from 3/4 of an hour to 1 hour.

RATAFIA SOUFFLÉ.

6 eggs, 2 oz. of Allinson fine wheatmeal, 2 oz. of butter, 2 oz. of castor sugar, the grated rind of 1/2 lemon, 1/2 pint of milk, 3 oz. of ratafias. Melt the butter in a saucepan, stir in the flour, mix well, and then add the milk, stirring all until the mixture is quite smooth and thick and comes away from the sides of the saucepan. Let it cool a little, then stir in the yolks of the

eggs well beaten, the lemon rind, the sugar, and lastly, the whites of the eggs whipped to a stiff froth. Turn the mixture into a buttered pie-dish or cake tin, with alternate layers of ratafias. Bake from 1/2 an hour to 3/4 of an hour in a moderately hot oven, and serve immediately with stewed fruit.

RICE SOUFFLÉ.

6 eggs, 2 oz. of rice, 1 pint of milk, sugar to taste, vanilla essence or the peel of 1/2 a lemon, and 1 oz. of butter. Stew the rice in the milk with the butter, sugar, and the lemon peel, if the latter is used for flavouring. When the rice is tender remove the peel; or flavour with vanilla essence, and let all cool. Separate the yolks of the eggs from the whites, and beat each separately into the rice for 2 or 3 minutes. Whip the whites of the eggs to a stiff froth, and stir them lightly into the mixture. Have ready a buttered Soufflé tin, pour the mixture into it, and bake the Soufflé for 20 minutes in a hot oven. Sprinkle with castor sugar, and serve at once.

SAVOURY CREAMED EGGS.

To each egg take 2 tablespoonfuls of cream or milk, a little chopped parsley, nutmeg, pepper, and salt to taste, and a slice of hot buttered toast. Butter the cups as in the last recipe, sprinkle well with parsley, beat up the eggs, season with nutmeg, pepper, and salt, and proceed as in "Sweet Creamed Eggs." Serve hot.

SAVOURY SOUFFLÉ.

4 eggs, 1 oz. Allinson fine wheatmeal, 1 gill of milk, 1 tablespoonful of finely chopped parsley, 1 dessertspoonful of finely minced spring onions, 1 oz. of butter, pepper and salt to taste. Proceed as in Cheese Soufflé, adding (instead of cheese) the parsley and onion.

SCALLOPED EGGS.

1/2 dozen hard-boiled eggs, 1/2 pint of milk, 1 dessertspoonful of Allinson fine wheatmeal, 1 oz. of cheese, 3 tablespoonfuls of brown breadcrumbs, and 1 oz. of butter. Shell and quarter the eggs; grease a shallow dish with part of the butter, and put the eggs in it. Make a thick sauce of the milk, wheatmeal, and cheese, adding seasoning to taste. Pour it over the eggs, cover with breadcrumbs; cut the rest of the butter in little pieces, and scatter them over the breadcrumbs. Bake till nicely browned.

SCOTCH EGGS.

5 hard-boiled eggs, 1 breakfastcupful of Allinson breadcrumbs, 1 Spanish onion, 1 teaspoonful of powdered sage, 1 dessertspoonful of finely chopped parsley, 1 egg, 1 oz. of butter, pepper and salt to taste, some oil, vege-butter, or butter for frying. Grate the onion, melt the butter, beat up the eggs, and mix them together with the breadcrumbs, herbs, and seasoning. Beat the forcemeat smooth, shell the eggs, cover them completely with a thick layer of forcemeat, and fry them a nice brown. Serve with brown gravy.

SPINACH TORTILLA.

4 eggs, 1 oz. of butter, a teacupful of boiled chopped spinach, lemon juice and pepper and salt to taste. Sprinkle the lemon juice over the spinach, and season well with pepper and salt, and fry it lightly in the butter. Beat the eggs and pour them into the mixture, let the tortilla set, then turn it with a plate, and set the other side. Serve hot.

STIRRED EGGS ON TOAST.

4 eggs, 1 oz. of butter, pepper and salt, 3 slices of hot buttered toast. Whip the eggs up well, add a dessertspoonful of water for each egg, and pepper and salt to taste. Heat the butter in a frying-pan, stir in the eggs over a mild fire. Keep stirring the mixture with a knife, removing the egg which sets round the sides and on the bottom of the frying-pan, and take the mixture from the fire directly it gets uniformly thick. It should not be allowed to cook until hard. Place the stirred eggs on the toast, and serve on a very hot dish. This quantity will suffice for 3 persons.

STUFFED EGGS.

4 hard-boiled eggs, 8 Spanish olives, 1/2 oz. of butter, pepper and salt to taste. Halve the eggs lengthway, and carefully remove the yolks. Pound these well, and mix them with the olives, which should be previously stoned and minced fine; add the butter and pepper and salt, and mix all well. Fill the whites of the eggs with the mixture. Pour some thick white sauce, flavoured with grated cheese, on a hot dish, and place the eggs on it. Serve hot.

SWEET CREAMED EGGS.

To each egg allow 2 tablespoonfuls of cream, or new milk, 1 teaspoonful of strawberry or raspberry and currant jam, 1 thin slice of buttered toast, sugar and vanilla to taste. Butter as many cups as eggs, reckoning 1 egg for each person. Place the jam in the centre of the cup; beat up the eggs with the cream or milk, sugar and vanilla, and divide the mixture into the cups. Cover each cup with buttered paper, stand the cups in a stew-pan with boiling water, which should reach only half-way up the cups, and steam the eggs until they are set—time from 8 to 10 minutes. Turn the eggs out on the buttered toast, and serve hot or cold.

SWISS EGGS.

4 eggs, 3 oz. of Gruyère cheese, 1 oz. of butter, 1 teaspoonful of finely chopped parsley, pepper and salt to taste. Spread the butter on a flat baking dish; lay on it some very thin slices of the cheese. On these break the eggs, keeping the yolks whole; grate the rest of the cheese, mix it with the parsley; strew this over the eggs, and bake them in a quick oven for 5 to 7 minutes.

TARRAGON EGGS.

4 hard-boiled eggs, 1/2 pint white sauce, 1 teaspoonful chopped tarragon, 1 tablespoonful tarragon vinegar, 2 yolks of eggs. Boil the eggs for 7 minutes, and cut them into slices. Lay them in a buttered pie-dish, have ready the sauce hot, and mix it into yolks, tarragon, and tarragon vinegar. Pour over the eggs, and bake for 10 minutes; serve with fried croûtons round.

TOMATO EGGS.

To each egg take 2 tablespoonfuls of tomato juice, which has been strained through a sieve; pepper and salt to taste. Batter a cup for each egg. Beat up the eggs, mix them with the tomato juice, season to taste, and divide into the buttered cups. Cover each cup with buttered paper, place them in a saucepan with boiling water, and steam the eggs for 10 minutes. Serve the eggs on buttered Allinson wholemeal toast.

TOMATO SOUFFLÉ.

4 eggs, 1 oz. of Allinson fine wheatmeal, 1/4 lb. of fresh tomatoes or a teacupful of tinned tomato, 1 oz. of butter, 1 clove of garlic or 2 shalots, pepper and salt to taste. Pulp the tomatoes through a sieve. Rub the garlic

round a small saucepan, and melt the butter, in it; or chop up very finely the shalots, and mix them with the butter. When the butter is hot, stir in the wheatmeal, then the tomato pulp, and stir until the mixture is thickened and comes away from the sides of the pan, then proceed as before, stirring in one yolk after the other; season with pepper and salt, whip up the whites of the eggs, stir them with the other ingredients, pour into a buttered Soufflé pan, and bake 15 minutes.

WATER EGGS.

4 eggs, 1-1/2 oz. of sugar, the rind and juice of 1/2 a lemon. Boil the sugar and lemon rind and juice in 1/2 pint of water for 15 minutes. Beat the eggs well, and add to them the sweetened water. Strain the mixture through a sieve into the dish in which it is to be served, place it in a larger dish with boiling water in a moderately hot oven, and bake until set. Serve hot or cold.

SALADS

These wholesome dishes are not used sufficiently by English people, for very few know the value of them. All may use these foods with benefit, and two dinners each week of them with Allinson wholemeal bread will prevent many a serious illness. They are natural food in a plain state, and supply the system with vegetable salts and acids in the best form. In winter, salads may be made with endive, mustard and cress, watercress, round lettuces, celery, or celery root, or even finely cut raw red or white cabbage; pepper, salt, oil, and vinegar are added as above. As a second course, milk or bread pudding. Salads are invaluable in cases of gout, rheumatism, gallstones, stone in the kidney or bladder, and in a gravelly condition of the water and impure condition of the system.

ARTICHOKE SALAD.

Boil potatoes and artichokes separately, cut into slices; mix, add pepper, salt, oil, and vinegar; eat with Allinson wholemeal bread.

CAULIFLOWER SALAD.

A medium-sized boiled cauliflower, 3 boiled potatoes, juice of 1/2 a lemon, 2 or 3 tablespoonfuls of oil. Cut up finely the cauliflower and potatoes when cold, mix well with the dressing, and pepper and salt to taste. A little mayonnaise is an improvement, but makes it rich.

CHEESE SALAD.

Put some finely shredded lettuce in a glass dish, and over this put some young sliced onions, some mustard and cress, a layer of sliced tomatoes, and two hard-boiled eggs, also sliced. Add salt and pepper, and then over all put a nice layer of grated cheese. Serve with a dressing composed of equal parts of cream, salad oil, and vinegar, into which had been smoothly mixed a little mustard.

CUCUMBER SALAD.

Peel and slice a cucumber, mix together 1/2 a teaspoonful of salt, 1/4 of a teaspoonful of white pepper, and 2 tablespoonfuls of olive oil, stir it well together, then add very gradually 1 tablespoonful of vinegar, stirring it all the time. Put the sliced cucumber into a salad dish, and garnish it with nasturtium leaves and flowers.

ONION SALAD.

1 large boiled Spanish onion, 3 large boiled potatoes, 1 teaspoonful of parsley, pepper and salt to taste, juice of 1 lemon, 2 or 3 tablespoonfuls of olive oil. Slice the onion and potatoes when quite cold, mix well together with the parsley and pepper and salt; add the lemon juice and oil, and mix well once more.

EGG MAYONNAISE.

4 medium-sized cold boiled potatoes, 6 hard-boiled eggs, 1 bunch of watercress, some mayonnaise. Slice the potatoes, and quarter the eggs. Arrange them in a dish, sprinkling pepper and salt in between; mix pieces of watercress with the eggs and tomatoes, pour over the mayonnaise, and garnish with more watercress.

POTATO SALAD (1).

Boil potatoes that are firm and waxy when cooked, and cut them in slices; let them soak in 1/2 gill of water, grate a small onion and mix it with these; add pepper, salt, vinegar, and oil to taste. The quantity of oil should be about three times the amount of the vinegar used. Eat with Allinson wholemeal bread.

POTATO SALAD (2).

1 lb. of cold boiled potatoes, 1 small beetroot, some spring onions, olives, 4 tablespoonfuls of vinegar, 2 of salad oil, a little tarragon vinegar, salt, pepper, minced parsley. Cut the potatoes in small pieces, put these into a salad bowl, cut up the onions and olives, and add them to the potatoes. Mix

the vinegar, oil, tarragon vinegar, salt, and pepper well together, pour it into the salad bowl, and stir it well. Garnish with beetroot and parsley.

SPANISH SALAD.

Put into the centre of the bowl some cold dressed French beans or scarlet runners, and before serving pour over some good mayonnaise. Garnish the beans with three tomatoes cut in slices and arranged in a circle one overlapping the other.

SUMMER SALAD.

1 large lettuce, 1 head endive, mustard and cress, watercress, 2 spring onions, 2 tomatoes, two hard-boiled eggs. Shred the lettuce, endive, onions, tomatoes, and cress, place in a salad bowl with mayonnaise dressing, decorate with slices of egg and tomato and tufts of cress.

SUMMER SALADS.

These are made from mixtures of lettuce, spring onions, cucumber, tomatoes, or any other raw or cooked green foods, pepper, salt, oil, and vinegar. Cold green peas, French beans, carrots, turnips, and lettuce make a good cold salad for the summer.

WINTER SALAD.

Cut up 1 lb. of cold boiled potatoes, grate fine 1 onion and mix with these, add watercress, or mustard and cress, and boiled and sliced beetroot; flavour with pepper, salt, oil, and vinegar as above. Hard-boiled eggs may be cut into slices and added, and sliced apples or pieces of orange may be advantageously mixed with the other ingredients.

When oranges are added to a salad the onion must be left out.

POTATO COOKERY

POTATO BIRD'S NEST.

A plateful of mashed potatoes, 2 lbs. of spinach well cooked and chopped, 3 hard-boiled eggs, 1 oz. of butter. Fry the mashed potatoes a nice brown in the butter, then place it on a dish in the shape of a ring. Inside this spread the spinach, and place the eggs, shelled, on the top of this. Serve as hot as possible.

POTATO CAKES

3 fair-sized potatoes, 1 egg, 2 tablespoonfuls of Allinson fine wheatmeal, pepper and salt to taste, and a pinch of nutmeg. Peel, wash, and grate the raw potatoes; beat up the egg and mix it with the potatoes, flour, and seasoning. Beat all well together, and fry the mixture like pancakes in oil or butter.

POTATO CHEESE.

6 oz. of mashed potatoes, 2 lemons, 6 oz. of sugar, 2 oz. of butter. Grate the rind of the lemons and pound it well with the sugar in a mortar, add the potatoes very finely mashed; oil the butter and mix this and the lemon juice with the rest of the ingredients; when all is very thoroughly mixed, fill the mixture in a jar and keep closely covered.

POTATO CHEESECAKES.

1 lb. of mashed potatoes, 4 oz. of grated cheese, 1 oz. of butter, 2 eggs, some bread raspings, 2 tablespoonfuls of Allinson fine wheatmeal, 1/2 a teaspoonful of mustard, pepper and salt to taste. Melt the butter and mix it with the mashed potatoes, add the cheese, flour, seasoning, mustard, and 1 of the eggs well beaten. Mix all well, and form the mixture into cakes. Beat up the second egg, turn the cakes into the beaten egg and raspings, and fry them in oil or butter until brown. Serve with tomato sauce and green vegetables.

POTATO CROQUETTES.

1/2 lb. of hot mashed potatoes, the yolks of 2 eggs, 1/2 a saltspoonful of nutmeg, pepper and salt, 1 whole egg, raspings, some Allinson nut-oil or butter for frying. Beat the potatoes well with the yolks of the eggs and the seasoning; form the mixture into balls; beat the egg well, roll the balls in the egg and breadcrumbs, and fry a nice brown.

POTATO PUDDING.

1 lb. of potatoes well mashed, 1 oz. of butter, 3 eggs, 1-1/2 oz. of sugar, the rind and juice of 1/2 a lemon, 1 gill of milk. Beat the butter, mix it with the mashed potatoes, add the eggs well beaten, also the other ingredients, turn the mixture into a buttered pie-dish, and bake it 1/2 hour.

POTATO PUFF.

1 pint of mashed potatoes, 2 oz. of butter, 3 eggs, 1/2 pint of milk, 1/2 a saltspoonful of nutmeg, pepper and salt to taste, and a dessertspoonful of finely chopped parsley. Beat the butter with a fork until it creams, mix the

potatoes with the butter, whip the yolks of the eggs well with the milk, and stir in the other ingredients. Add the nutmeg, parsley, and seasoning, and last of all the whites of the eggs, beaten to a stiff froth. The potatoes, butter, eggs, and milk should be well beaten separately before being used, as the success of the dish depends on this. Turn the mixture into a buttered pie-dish, and bake it for 1 hour in a hot oven.

POTATO ROLLS (BAKED).

2 lbs. of cold mashed potatoes, 1 boiled Spanish onion, 1 oz. of butter, the yolk of 1 egg, a little nutmeg, pepper and salt to taste, and a teaspoonful of powdered thyme. Chop up the onion fine, and mix it with the mashed potatoes. Warm the butter until melted, and add this, the yolk of egg, and the thyme. Mix all well, make the mixture into little rolls 3 inches long, brush them over with a pastry brush dipped in Allinson nut-oil or hot butter and bake them on a floured tin until brown, which will take from 10 to 20 minutes. Serve with brown sauce and vegetables.

POTATO ROLLS (Spanish).

3 teacupfuls of mashed potatoes, 3 tablespoonfuls of Allinson fine wheatmeal, 18 olives, 1 egg well beaten; seasoning to taste. Stone the olives and chop them up fine, mix the meal, mashed potato, olive, and egg well together, season with pepper and salt; add a little milk if necessary, make the mixture into rolls, and proceed as in "Potato Rolls."

POTATO SALAD (1).

4 medium-sized cold boiled potatoes, 1 small onion minced very fine, 1 dessertspoonful of finely chopped parsley, oil and lemon juice, pepper and salt to taste. Slice the potatoes, let them soak with 3 tablespoonfuls of water,

mix them with the onion and parsley, and dress like any other salad. Any good salad dressing may be used.

POTATO SALAD (2).

1-1/2 pints of mashed potatoes, 2 hard-boiled eggs, 2 tablespoonfuls of Allinson salad oil, 1/2 a teacupful of milk, 1 teaspoonful of mustard, pepper, salt, and lemon juice to taste. Make a dressing of the oil, milk, mustard, and seasoning. Mash the yolks of the eggs and mix them with the lemon juice, and add this to the dressing. Chop the whites of the eggs up fine. Mix the mashed potatoes, dressing, and chopped whites of eggs well together. Turn the mixture into a salad bowl or glass dish, and garnish with parsley or watercress and beetroot.

POTATO SALAD (MASHED).

1/2 pint of mashed potatoes, 2 hard-boiled eggs, 2 tablespoonfuls of Allinson salad oil, 1 dessertspoonful of sugar, 1 teaspoonful of mustard, pepper and salt to taste, 2 tablespoonfuls of lemon juice and seasoning; mash the yolks of the eggs quite fine and mix them smooth with the lemon juice, and add this to the dressing. Chop the whites of the eggs up very fine, mix all together; turn the mixture smoothly into a salad bowl or glass dish, and garnish with watercress and beetroot.

POTATO SAUSAGES.

1 pint of mashed potato, 2 eggs well beaten, 1 breakfastcupful of breadcrumbs, 2 oz. of butter (or Allinson nut-oil), 1/2 a saltspoonful of nutmeg, pepper and salt. Mash the potatoes well with one of the eggs, add seasoning, form the mixture into sausages, roll them in egg and breadcrumbs, and fry them brown.

POTATO SNOW (a Pretty Dish).

1-1/2 lbs. of potatoes, 3 hard-boiled eggs, 1 small beetroot. Boil the potatoes till tender, pass them through a potato masher into a hot dish, letting the mashed potato fall lightly, and piling it up high. Slice the eggs and beetroot, and arrange alternate slices of egg and beetroot round the base of the potato snow. Brown the top with a salamander, or, if such is not handy, with a coal-shovel made red hot.

POTATO SURPRISE.

1 pint of mashed potatoes, 1 oz. of butter, 4 tomatoes, pepper and salt, 1 tablespoonful of finely chopped parsley. Mix the butter well with the mashed potatoes, season with a little pepper and salt. Butter 8 patty pans and line them with a thick layer of potato; place 1/2 a tomato in each, with a little of the parsley and a dusting of pepper and salt. Cover with mashed potatoes, and brown the patties in the oven.

POTATO WITH CHEESE.

1 pint of finely mashed potatoes, 1/2 oz. of butter, 3 oz. of grated cheese, a little nutmeg, pepper and salt to taste. Mix all well with the seasoning, grease some patty pans, fill them with the mixture, and bake them in a moderate oven until golden brown. Serve with vegetables and any savoury sauce.

POTATOES À LA DUCHESSE.

Prepare potatoes as in "Milk Potatoes," leaving out the parsley; beat up, 1 egg with the juice of 1 lemon, let the potatoes go off the boil, add the egg and lemon juice carefully; re-heat the whole again but do not allow it to boil, to avoid the egg curdling.

POTATOES (BROWNED).

1 pint of mashed potato, 1 large English onion, 1 oz. of butter, pepper and salt. Mince the onion very fine and fry it a golden brown in the butter, mix it well with the mashed potato, and add seasoning to taste; form the mixture into cakes, flour them well, place them in a greased baking tin, with little bits of butter on the top of the cakes, and bake them a nice brown.

POTATOES AND CARROTS.

1-1/2 lbs. of boiled potatoes, 3/4 lb. of boiled carrots, 2 eggs, 1 oz. of butter pepper and salt to taste, some Parsley. Mash the potatoes and carrots together, beat the eggs well and mix them with the vegetables, add seasoning; butter a mould, fill it with the mixture, spread the butter on the top, bake the whole for 1/2 hour, turn out, and garnish with parsley.

POTATOES (CURRIED).

6 good-sized potatoes parboiled, 1 oz. of butter, 1 teaspoonful of curry powder, 3/4 pint of milk, 1 dessertspoonful of fine wheatmeal, salt and lemon juice to taste. Slice the potatoes into a saucepan and pour the milk over them; smooth the curry powder with a little water, pour this over the potatoes, and add the butter and seasoning. Let the potatoes cook gently until soft; then thicken with the meal, which should be previously smoothed with a little milk or water. Let all simmer for 2 or 3 minutes; add lemon juice, and serve.

POTATOES (MASHED).

To mash potatoes well they should be drained when soft and steamed dry over the fire; then turn them into a basin and pass them through a potato masher back into the saucepan; add a piece of butter the size of a walnut (or more according to quantity of potatoes), and a little hot milk, and mash all well through over the fire with a wooden spoon, adding hot milk as required until it is a thick, creamy mass.

POTATOES (MASHED)(another way).

1 finely chopped English onion to 1 pound of potatoes, piece of butter the size of a walnut, pepper and salt to taste. Fry the onion a nice brown in the butter, taking care not to burn it. When the potatoes have been passed through the masher back into the saucepan, add the fried onion and seasoning and a little hot milk. Mash all well through, and serve very hot.

POTATOES (MILK).

Boil or steam potatoes in their skins; when soft, peel and slice them. Make a sauce of milk, thickened with Allinson fine wheatmeal, and season with pepper and salt. Let the potatoes simmer in the sauce for 10 minutes. Before serving mix into the sauce a spoonful of finely chopped parsley.

POTATOES (MILK) WITH CAPERS.

1 lb. of potatoes, 3/4 pint of milk, 1 tablespoonful of finely chopped capers, 1 teaspoonful of vinegar, pepper and salt to taste, 1 tablespoonful of Allinson wholemeal, boil the potatoes till nearly tender; drain them and cut

them in slices. Return them to the saucepan, add the milk and seasoning, and when the milk boils add the wheatmeal. Let all simmer until the potatoes are tender, add the capers and vinegar. Then simmer a few minutes with the capers, and serve.

POTATOES (SAVOURY).

1-1/2 lbs. of small boiled potatoes, 1 oz. of butter, 1 dessertspoonful of finely chopped onion, 3 eggs, 1 dessertspoonful of vinegar, pepper and salt to taste, 1 clove of garlic. Slice the potatoes into the saucepan and let them stew gently for 15 minutes with the butter, onion, and seasoning, shaking them occasionally to prevent burning. Rub the inside of a basin with the garlic, break the eggs into it, beat them well with the vinegar, and pour them over the potatoes, shake the whole well over the fire until thoroughly mixed, and serve.

POTATOES (SCALLOPED).

6 medium-sized boiled potatoes, 2 onions chopped fine, and fried brown, 1 breakfastcupful of milk, 1 oz. of butter, pepper and salt, a little Allinson wholemeal. Slice the potatoes; butter a pie-dish, put into it a layer of potatoes, over this sprinkle pepper and salt, some of the onion, part of the butter, and a little meal. Repeat this until the dish is full, pour the milk over the whole, and bake for 1 hour.

POTATOES (STUFFED) (1).

6 large potatoes, 1-1/2 breakfastcupfuls of breadcrumbs, 1/2 lb. of grated English onions, 1 teaspoonful of powdered sage, 1 ditto of finely chopped parsley, 1 egg well beaten, piece of butter the size of a walnut, pepper and salt to taste. Halve the potatoes, scoop them out, leaving nearly 1 inch of the

inside all round. Make a stuffing of the other ingredients, adding a very little milk it the stuffing should be too dry; fill the potatoes with it, tie the halves together, and bake them until done. Serve with brown sauce.

POTATOES (STUFFED)(2).

6 large potatoes, 1 Spanish onion, 1 large apple, 1 oz. of butter, 1/2 teaspoonful of allspice, 1 dessertspoonful of sugar, pepper and salt to taste, a cupful of breadcrumbs. Chop the onion and apple fine and stew them (without water) with the butter, allspice, sugar, and seasoning. When quite tender sift in enough breadcrumbs to make a fairly stiff paste. Scoop the potatoes out as in previous recipe, fill them with the mixture, tie, bake the potatoes till tender, and serve them with brown sauce and vegetables.

POTATOES (STUFFED) (3).

6 large boiled potatoes, 1-1/2 ozs. of grated Gruyère or Canadian cheese, 1 egg well beaten, pepper and salt to taste, a piece of butter the size of a walnut. Halve the potatoes as before, scoop them out, leaving 1/2 inch of potato wall all round. Mash the scooped out potato well up with the cheese, add the egg, butter, and seasoning, also a little milk if necessary; fill the potatoes, tie them together, brush over with a little oiled butter, and bake them 10 to 15 minutes. Serve with vegetables and white sauce.

POTATOES (STUFFED) (4).

6 large boiled potatoes, 1 large English onion, 1/2 oz. of butter, 1 egg well beaten, pepper and salt to taste. Halve the potatoes as before, scoop out most of the soft part and mash it up. Mince the onion very finely and fry it a nice brown with the best part of the butter, mix all up together, adding the egg and seasoning, fill the potato skins, tie the halves together, brush them

over with the rest of the butter (oiled), and put them in the oven until well heated through. Serve with vegetables and brown sauce.

POTATOES (TOASTED).

Cut cold boiled potatoes into slices, brush them over with oiled butter, place them on a gridiron (if not handy, in a wire salad basket), and put it over a clear fire. Brown the slices on both sides.

SAUCES

Flesh-eaters have the gravy of meat to eat with their vegetables, and when they give up the use of flesh they are often at a loss for a good substitute. Sauces may be useful in more ways than one. When not too highly spiced or seasoned they help to prevent thirst, as they supply the system with fluid, and when made with the liquor in which vegetables have been boiled they retain many valuable salts which would otherwise have been lost. When foods are eaten in a natural condition no sauces are required, but when food is changed by cooking many persons require it to be made more appetising, as it is called. The use of sauces is thus seen to be an aid to help down plain and wholesome food, and being fluid they cause the food to be more thoroughly broken up and made into a porridgy mass before it is swallowed. From a health point of view artificial sauces are not good, but if made as I direct very little harm will result.

Brown Gravy, Fried Onion Sauce, or Herb Gravy must be used with great caution, or not at all by those who are troubled with heartburn, acidity, biliousness, or skin eruptions of any kind.

The water in which vegetables (except cabbage or potatoes) have been boiled is better for making sauces than ordinary water.

APPLE SAUCE.

1 lb. of apples, 1 gill of water, 1-1/2 oz. of sugar (or more, according to taste), 1/2 a teaspoonful of mixed spice. Pare and core the apples, cut them up, and cook them with the water until quite mashed up, add sugar and spice. Rub the apples through a sieve, re-heat, and serve. Can also be served cold.

APRICOT SAUCE.

1/2 lb. of apricot jam, 1/2 a teaspoonful of Allinson cornflour. Dilute the jam with 1/2 pint of water, boil it up and pass it through a sieve; boil the sauce up, and thicken it with the cornflour. Serve hot or cold.

BOILED ONION SAUCE.

This is made as "Wheatmeal Sauce," but plenty of boiled and chopped onions are mixed in it. This goes well with any plain vegetables.

BROWN GRAVY.

Put a tablespoonful of butter or olive oil into a frying-pan or saucepan, make it hot, dredge in a tablespoonful of Allinson fine wheatmeal, brown this, then add boiling water, with pepper and salt to taste. A little mushroom or walnut ketchup may be added it desired. Eat with vegetables or savouries.

BROWN SAUCE (1).

1 oz. of Allinson fine wheatmeal, 1 oz. of butter, the juice of 1/2 a lemon, a blade of mace, pepper and salt to taste. Melt the butter in a frying-pan over the fire, stir into it the meal, and keep on stirring until it is a brown colour. Stir in gradually enough boiling water to make the sauce of the thickness of cream. Add the lemon juice, the mace, and seasoning, and let the sauce simmer for 20 minutes. Remove the mace, and pour the sauce over the onions. If the sauce should be lumpy, strain it through a gravy-strainer.

BROWN SAUCE (2).

2 tablespoonfuls of Allinson fine wheatmeal, 1 oz. of butter, 6 eschalots chopped fine, 3 bay leaves, 1/2 a lemon (peeled) cut in slices, pepper and salt to taste. Brown the meal with the butter; add water enough to make the sauce the thickness of cream; add the eschalots, lemon, bay leaves, and seasoning. Let all simmer 15 to 20 minutes; strain, return the sauce to the saucepan, and boil it up before serving.

CAPER SAUCE.

Leave out the onions, otherwise make as "Wheatmeal Sauce." Add capers, and cook 10 minutes after adding them. This goes very well with plain boiled macaroni, or macaroni batter, or macaroni with turnips, &c.

CHOCOLATE SAUCE.

1 bar of Allinson chocolate, 1/2 pint of milk, 1/2 teaspoonful of cornflour, 1/2 teaspoonful of vanilla essence. Melt the chocolate over the fire with 1 tablespoonful of water, add the milk, and stir well; when it boils add the cornflour and vanilla. Boil the sauce up, and serve.

CURRANT SAUCE (RED & WHITE).

1/2 pint of both white and red currants, 2 ozs. of sugar, 1 gill of water, 1/2 a teaspoonful of cornflour. Cook the ingredients for 10 minutes, rub the fruit through a sieve, re-heat it, and thicken the sauce with the cornflour. Serve hot or cold.

CURRY SAUCE (1).

3 English onions, 1 carrot, 1 good cooking apple, 1 teaspoonful of curry powder, 1/2 oz. of butter, 1 dessertspoonful of Allinson fine wheatmeal, salt to taste. Chop up the onions, carrot, and apple, and stew them in 3/4 pint of water until quite tender, adding the curry and salt. When quite soft rub the vegetables well through a sieve; brown the meal in the saucepan in the butter, add the sauce to this, and let it simmer for a few minutes; add a little more water if necessary.

CURRY SAUCE (2).

1 onion, 1 even teaspoonful of curry, 1/2 pint of water, 1/2 oz. of butter, 1 teaspoonful of Allinson fine wheatmeal, a little burnt sugar. Grate the onion into the water, add curry, butter, and salt, and let these ingredients cook a few minutes. Thicken the sauce with the meal, and colour with burnt sugar.

CURRY SAUCE (BROWN).

2 tablespoonfuls of Allinson fine wheatmeal, 1 oz. of butter (or oil), 1 teaspoonful of curry powder, 1 English onion chopped fine, 1 good tablespoonful of vinegar, a pinch of mint and sage, and salt to taste. Fry the onions in the butter until nearly brown, add the meal, and brown; add as much water as required to make the sauce the consistency of cream; add the curry, vinegar, and seasoning. Let the whole simmer for 5 to 10 minutes, strain the sauce, return to the saucepan, beat it up, and serve.

EGG CAPER SAUCE.

The same as "Egg Sauce," adding 1 tablespoonful of finely chopped capers before the egg is stirred in, and which should simmer a few minutes.

EGG SAUCE.

3/4 pint of half milk and water, 1 egg, 1 teaspoonful of Allinson cornflour, juice of 1/2 lemon, 1/2 oz. of butter, pepper and salt. Boil the milk and water, add the butter and seasoning. Thicken the sauce with the cornflour; beat the egg up with the lemon juice. Let the sauce go off the boil; add gradually and gently the egg, taking care not to curdle it. Warm up the sauce again, but do not allow it to boil.

EGG SAUCE WITH SAFFRON.

1/2 pint of milk and water, 1 egg, 1 teaspoonful of cornflour, a pinch of saffron, pepper and salt to taste. Boil the milk and water with the saffron, and see that the latter dissolves thoroughly. Add seasoning, and thicken with the cornflour; beat up the egg, and after having allowed the sauce to cool a little, add it gradually, taking care not to curdle the sauce. Heat it up, but do not let it boil. To easily dissolve the saffron, it should be dried in the oven and then powdered.

FRENCH SAUCE.

1 oz. of butter, 2 oz. each of carrot, turnip, onion, or eschalots, 1 tablespoonful of vinegar, 1 dessertspoonful of Allinson fine wheatmeal, pepper and salt to taste, a little thyme. Chop the vegetables up fine, and fry them in the butter, adding the thyme. When slightly browned add 3/4 pint of water, into which the meal has been rubbed smooth. Stir the sauce until it boils, then add the vinegar and seasoning. Let all simmer for 1/2 an hour, rub the sauce through a sieve, return it to the saucepan, boil up, and serve.

FRIED ONION SAUCE.

Chop fine an onion, fry, add Allinson fine wheatmeal, and make into a sauce like brown gravy.

HERB SAUCE.

Make like "Brown Gravy," and add mixed herbs a little before serving.

HORSERADISH SAUCE.

1/2 pint of water, 2 tablespoonfuls of grated horseradish, 1 dessertspoonful of Allinson fine wheatmeal, 1/2 oz. butter, salt to taste. Boil the water, butter, and horseradish for a few minutes, add salt, and thicken the sauce with the meal rubbed smooth in a little cold water; cook for two minutes, and serve.

MAYONNAISE SAUCE.

1/2 pint of oil, the yolk of 1 egg, the juice of a lemon, 1/2 teaspoonful each of mustard, pepper, and salt. Place the yolks in a basin, which should be quite cold; work them smooth with a wooden spoon, add the salt, pepper, and mustard, and mix all well. Stir in the oil very gradually, drop by drop; when the sauce begins to thicken stir in a little of the lemon juice, continue with the oil, and so on alternately until the sauce is finished. Be sure to make it in a cool place, also to stir one way only. It you follow directions the sauce may curdle; should this ever happen, do not waste the curdled sauce, but start afresh with a fresh yolk of egg, stirring in a little fresh oil first, and then adding the curdled mixture.

MILK FROTH SAUCE.

1/2 pint of milk, 2 eggs, sugar to taste, some essence of vanilla or any other flavouring, 1 teaspoonful of Allinson fine wheatmeal. Mix the milk, eggs, flour, and flavouring, and proceed as in "Orange Froth Sauce."

MINT SAUCE.

1 teacupful of vinegar, 1 teacupful of water, 1 tablespoonful of sugar, 1 heaped-up tablespoonful of finely chopped mint. Mix all the ingredients well, and let the sauce soak at least 1 hour before serving.

MUSTARD SAUCE.

1 good teaspoonful of mustard, 1 dessertspoonful of Allinson fine wheatmeal, 1 oz. of butter, vinegar and salt to taste, 1 teaspoonful of sugar, 1/2 pint of water. Brown the wheatmeal with the butter in the saucepan, add the mustard, vinegar, sugar, and salt, let all simmer for a few minutes, and then serve.

OLIVE SAUCE.

Make a white sauce, stone and chop 8 Spanish olives, add them to the sauce, and let it cook a few minutes before serving.

ONION SAUCE.

1 large Spanish onion, 1/2 pint of milk, 1 gill of water, 4 oz. of butter, 1 dessertspoonful of Allinson fine wheatmeal, pepper and salt to taste. Chop

the onions up fine, and cook them in the water until tender, add the milk, butter and seasoning. Smooth the meal with a little water, thicken the sauce, let it simmer for five minutes, and serve.

ORANGE FLOWER SAUCE

Make a sweet white sauce, and flavour it with 2 tablespoonfuls of orangeflower water.

ORANGE FROTH SAUCE.

The juice of 2 oranges, 2 eggs, sugar to taste, 1 teaspoonful of white flour (not cornflour), add to the orange juice enough water to make 1/2 pint of liquid; mix this well with the sugar, the eggs previously beaten, and the flour smoothed with a very little water; put the mixture over the fire in an enamelled saucepan, and whisk it well until quite frothy; do not allow the sauce to boil, as it would then be spoiled. Serve immediately.

ORANGE SAUCE

2 oranges, 4 large lumps of sugar, 1/2 a teaspoonful of cornflour, some water. Rub the sugar on the rind of one of the oranges until all the yellow part is taken off; take the juice of both the oranges and add it to the sugar. Mix smooth the cornflour in 8 tablespoonfuls of water, add this to the juice when hot, and stir the sauce over the fire until thickened; serve at once.

PARSLEY SAUCE.

This is made as "Wheatmeal Sauce," but some finely chopped parsley is added five minutes before serving.

RASPBERRY FROTH SAUCE.

1/2 pint of raspberries, 1 gill of water, 2 eggs, sugar to taste, 1 teaspoonful of white flour. Boil the raspberries in the water for 10 minutes, then strain through a cloth or fine hair sieve; add a little more water if the juice is not 1/2 pint; allow it to get cold, then add the eggs, flour, and sugar, and proceed as for "Orange Froth Sauce." This sauce can be made with any kind of fruit juice.

RATAFIA SAUCE.

3 oz. of ratafias, 1/2 pint of milk; the yolk of 1 egg. Bruise the ratafias and put them in a stewpan with the milk; let it boil, remove from the fire, beat up the yolk of egg, and when the milk has cooled a little stir it in carefully; stir again over the fire until the sauce has thickened a little, but do not let it boil.

ROSE SAUCE.

Make a sweet white sauce, and flavour with 2 tablespoonfuls of rosewater.

SAVOURY SAUCE.

1 onion, 3 carrots, 1 oz. butter, a teaspoonful of Allinson fine wheatmeal, a little nutmeg, pepper and salt to taste. Chop up the onion and fry it a nice brown; cut up the carrots into small dice, cook them gently in 1 pint of water with the onion and seasoning until quite soft; then rub the sauce

through a sieve, return it to the saucepan, heat it up and thicken it with the meal, if necessary.

SORREL SAUCE.

Make a white sauce, and add to it a handful of finely chopped sorrel; let it simmer a few minutes, and serve.

SPICE SAUCE.

Make a sweet white sauce, and add 1/2 teaspoonful of mixed spice before serving.

TARTARE SAUCE.

1 lb. of mushrooms, 1 small onion, 1/2 oz. of butter, 1 dessertspoonful of Allinson fine wheatmeal, pepper and salt to taste, juice of 1/2 a lemon. Cook the mushrooms and onion, chopped fine, in 1/2 pint of water for 15 minutes; adding the butter and seasoning. Strain the sauce and return it to the saucepan, thicken it with the meal, add the lemon juice, let it simmer 2 or 3 minutes, and serve.

TOMATO SAUCE (1).

1/2 a canful of tinned tomatoes or 1 lb. of fresh ones, a tablespoonful of Allinson fine wheatmeal, 1/2 oz. of butter, pepper and salt to taste. If fresh tomatoes are used, slice them and set them to cook with a breakfastcupful of water. For tinned tomatoes a teacupful of water is sufficient. Let the tomatoes cook gently for 10 minutes, then rub them well through a strainer.

Return the liquid to the saucepan, add the butter, pepper, and salt, and when it boils thicken the sauce with the meal, which should he smoothed well with a little cold water. Let the sauce simmer for a minute, and pour it into a warm sauce-boat.

TOMATO SAUCE (2).

Cut up fresh or tinned tomatoes, cook with water and finely chopped onions; when done rub through a sieve, boil up again, thicken with Allinson fine wheatmeal made into a paste with water. Add a little butter, pepper, and salt. Eat with vegetables or savoury dishes.

WHEATMEAL SAUCE.

Mix milk and water together in equal proportions, add a grated onion, and boil; rub a little Allinson fine wheatmeal into a paste with cold water. Mix this with the boiling milk and water, and let it thicken; add a little pepper and salt to taste. Eat this with vegetables.

WHITE SAUCE (1).

3/4 pint of milk, 1 dessertspoonful of Allinson fine wheatmeal, sugar to taste. Boil 1/2 pint of the milk with sugar, mix the meal smooth in the rest of the milk, add this to the boiling milk and keep stirring until the sauce has thickened, cook for 3 to 4 minutes, strain it through a gravy strainer, re-heat, and flavour with vanilla or almond essence.

WHITE SAUCE (2).

1/2 pint of milk, a dessertspoonful of Allinson cornflour or potato flour, a little vanilla essence, 1 teaspoonful of sugar. Boil the milk, thicken it with the cornflour previously smoothed with a little water, add sugar and vanilla, boil up, and serve with the pudding.

WHITE SAUCE (SAVOURY).

3/4 pint of milk, 1 good dessertspoonful of Allinson fine wheatmeal, a small piece of butter, size of a nut, pepper and salt to taste. Bring part of the milk to the boil, mix the meal smooth with the rest, add the butter and seasoning, and thicken the sauce. Let it cook gently a few minutes after adding the meal, and serve.

PUDDINGS

ALMOND PUDDING (1).

4 eggs, 3 oz. of castor sugar, 4 oz. of ground sweet almonds, 1/2 oz. of ground bitter almonds. Whip the whites of the eggs to a stiff froth, mix them lightly with the well-beaten yolks, add the other ingredients gradually. Have ready a well-buttered pie-dish, pour the mixture in (not filling the dish more than three-quarters full), and bake in a moderately hot oven until a knitting needle pushed through comes out clean. Turn the pudding out and serve cold.

ALMOND PUDDING (2).

1/2 lb. of almond paste, 1/4 lb. of butter, 2 eggs, 2 tablespoonfuls of sifted sugar, cream, and ratafia flavouring. With a spoonful of water make the ground almonds into a paste, warm the butter, mix the almonds with this, and add the sugar and 2 tablespoonfuls of cream or milk, and the eggs well beaten. Mix well, and butter some cups, half fill them, and bake the puddings for about 20 minutes. Turn them out on a dish, and serve with sweet sauce.

ALMOND RICE.

1/2 lb. of rice, 2-1/2 pints of milk, 1 oz. of butter, 3 oz. of ground sweet almonds and a dozen bitter ground almonds, sugar to taste, 1 teaspoonful of cinnamon, some raspberry jam. Cook the rice, butter, milk, sugar, and almonds until the rice is quite tender, which will take from 40 to 50 minutes; butter a mould, sift the cinnamon over it evenly, pour in the rice, let it get cold, turn out and serve with sauce made of raspberry jam and water. Dip the mould into hot water for 1/2 a minute, if the rice will not turn out easily.

APPLE CHARLOTTE.

2 lbs. of cooking apples, 1 teacupful of mixed currants and sultanas, 1 heaped up teaspoonful of ground cinnamon, 2 oz. of blanched and chopped almonds, sugar to taste, Allinson wholemeal bread, and butter. Pare, core, and cut up the apples and set them to cook with 1 teacupful of water. Some apples require much more water than others. When they are soft, add the fruit picked and washed, the cinnamon, and the almonds and sugar. Cut very thin slices of bread and butter, line a buttered pie-dish with them. Place a layer of apples over the buttered bread, and repeat the layers of bread and apples until the dish is full, finishing with a layer of bread and butter. Bake from 3/4 hour to 1 hour.

APRICOT PUDDING.

1 tin of apricots, 6 sponge cakes, 1/2 pint of milk, 2 eggs. Put the apricots into a saucepan, and let them simmer with a little sugar for 1/2 an hour; take them off the fire and beat them with a fork. Mix with them the sponge cakes crumbled. Beat the eggs up with milk and pour it on the apricots. Pour the mixture into a wetted mould and bake in a hot oven with a cover over the mould for 1/2 an hour. Turn out; serve either hot or cold.

BAKED CUSTARD PUDDING.

1 pint of milk, 3 eggs, sugar, vanilla flavouring, nutmeg. Warm the milk, beat up the eggs with the sugar, pour the milk over, and flavour. Have a pie-

dish lined at the edge with baked paste, strain the custard into the dish, grate a little nutmeg over the top, and bake in a slow oven for 1/2 an hour. Serve in the pie-dish with stewed rhubarb.

BARLEY (PEARL) AND APPLE PUDDING.

1/2 lb. of pearl barley, 1 lb. of apples, 2 oz. of sugar, 1/4 oz. of butter, the grated rind of a lemon. Soak the barley overnight, and boil it in 3 pints of water for 3 hours. When quite tender, add the sugar, lemon rind, and the apples pared, cored, and chopped fine. Pour the mixture into a buttered dish, put the butter in bits over the top, and bake for 1 hour.

BATTER JAM PUDDING.

1 pint of milk, 3 oz. of cornflour, 3 oz. of Allinson fine wheatmeal, 2 oz. of butter, 3 eggs, some raspberry or apricot jam. Rub the cornflour and meal smooth with a little of the milk; bring the rest to boil with the butter, and stir into it the smooth paste. Stir the mixture over the fire for about 8 minutes, then turn it into a basin to cool. Beat up the yolks of the eggs and add them to the cooked batter; whip the whites of the eggs to a stiff froth and add them to the rest; butter a pie-dish, pour in a layer of the batter, then spread a layer of jam, and so on, until the dish is full, finishing with the batter, and bake the pudding for 1/2 an hour.

BATTER PUDDING.

1/2 lb. of Allinson fine wheatmeal, 1 pint of milk, 3 eggs, 1 dessertspoonful of sugar, 1 teaspoonful of ground cinnamon (or any other flavouring preferred). Beat the eggs well, mix all thoroughly, and bake about 3/4 hour.

BELGIAN PUDDING.

Soak a 1d. French roll in 1/2 pint of boiling milk; for 1 hour, then add 1/4 lb. of sultanas, 1/4 lb. of currants, 3 oz. of sugar, 4 chopped apples, a little chopped peel, the yolks of 3 eggs, a little grated nutmeg and zest of lemon. Mix in lastly the whites of the 3 eggs whisked to a stiff froth, pour into a mould, and boil for 2 hours. Serve with a sweet sauce.

BIRD-NEST PUDDING.

6 medium-sized apples, 5 eggs, 1 quart of milk, sugar, the rind of 1/2 a lemon and some almond or vanilla essence. Pare and core the apples, and boil them in 1 pint of water, sweetened with 2 oz. of sugar, and the lemon rind added, until they are beginning to get soft. Remove the apples from the saucepan and place them in a pie-dish without the syrup. Heat the milk and make a custard with the eggs, well beaten, and the hot milk; sweeten and flavour it to taste, pour the custard over the apples, and bake the pudding until the custard is set.

BREAD AND JAM PUDDING.

Fill a greased pudding basin with slices of Allinson bread, each slice spread thickly with raspberry jam; make a custard by dissolving 1 tablespoonful of cornflour in 1 pint of milk well beaten; boil up and pour this over the jam and bread; let it stand 1 hour; then boil for 1 hour covered with a pudding cloth. Serve either hot or cold, turned out of the basin.

BREAD PUDDING (STEAMED).

3/4 lb. of breadcrumbs, 1 wineglassful of rosewater, 1 pint of milk, 3 oz. of ground almonds, sugar to taste, 4 eggs well beaten, 1 oz. of butter (oiled).

Mix all the ingredients, and let them soak for 1/2 an hour. Turn into a buttered mould and steam the pudding for 1-1/2 to 2 hours.

BREAD SOUFFLÉ.

5 oz. of Allinson wholemeal bread, 1 pint of milk, 2 tablespoonfuls of orange or rosewater, sugar to taste, 4 eggs. Soak the bread in the milk until perfectly soft; add sugar and the rose or orange water; beat the mixture up with the yolks of the eggs; beat the whites of the eggs to a stiff froth, and mix them lightly with the rest; pour the whole into a well-buttered pie-dish and bake the Soufflé for 1/2 an hour in a brisk oven; serve immediately.

BUCKINGHAM PUDDING.

1/4 lb. of ratafias, 4 or 5 sponge cakes, 3 eggs, 3/4 pint of milk, sugar to taste, vanilla flavouring. Butter a mould, press the ratafias all over it, and lay in the sponge cakes cut in slices; then put in more ratafias and sponge cakes until the mould is almost full. Beat the yolks of the eggs well together and the whites of 2 eggs. Boil the milk and pour it on the eggs, let it cool a little, add sugar and flavouring. Pour into the mould. Cover it with buttered paper and steam for about 1 hour. Turn it out carefully, and serve with jam or sauce round it.

BUN PUDDING.

3 stale 1d. buns, 1-1/2 pints milk, 3 eggs, 2 oz. sugar. Cut the buns in thin slices, put them in a dish, beat the eggs well, add to the milk and sugar, and pour over the buns; cover with a plate, then stand for 2 hours; bake for 1 hour in a moderate oven, or steam for 1-1/2 hours, as preferred; serve with lemon sauce.

CABINET PUDDING (1).

1/2 lb. of Allinson bread cut in thin slices, eggs and milk as in Bun Pudding, 1 breakfastcupful of currants and sultanas mixed, 1 heaped-up teaspoonful of cinnamon, 2 oz. of butter, 2 oz. of chopped almonds, and sugar to taste. Soak the bread as directed in above recipe, add the fruit, which should be previously well washed, picked, and dried, and the cinnamon, almonds, and sugar. Dissolve part of the butter, add it to the rest of the ingredients, and mix them all well together. Butter a pie-dish with the rest of the butter, and bake the pudding in a moderate oven for 1 hour.

CABINET PUDDING (2).

2 oz. dried cherries, 2 oz. citron peel, 2 oz. ratafias, 8 stale sponge cakes, 1 pint of milk, 4 eggs, well beaten, a few drops of almond essence, and some raspberry jam. Butter a mould and decorate it with the cherries and citron cut into fine strips, break up the sponge cakes and fill the mould with layers of sponge cake, ratafias, and jam. When the mould is nearly full, pour over the mixture the custard of milk and eggs with the flavouring added. Steam the pudding for 1 hour, and serve with sauce.

CABINET PUDDING (3).

Butter a pint pudding mould and decorate it with preserved cherries, then fill the basin with layers of sliced sponge cakes and macaroons, scattering a few cherries between the layers. Make a pint of custard with Allinson custard powder, add to it 2 tablespoonfuls of raisin wine and pour over the cakes, &c., steam the pudding carefully for three-quarters of an hour, taking care not to let the water boil into it; serve with wine sauce.

CANADIAN PUDDING.

To use up cold stiff porridge. Mix the porridge with enough hot milk to make it into a fairly thick batter. Beat up 1 or 2 eggs, 1 egg to a breakfastcupful of the batter, add some jam, stirring it well into the batter, bake 1 hour in a buttered pie-dish.

CARROT PUDDING.

3 large carrots, 3 eggs, 1/2 pint of milk, 4 oz. of Allinson fine wheatmeal, 2 tablespoonfuls of syrup, 1 teaspoonful of cinnamon. Scrape and grate the carrots, make a batter of the other ingredients, add the grated carrots, pour the mixture into a buttered mould, and steam the pudding for 2-1/2 to 3 hours.

CHOCOLATE ALMOND PUDDING.

1/2 lb. of ground sweet almonds, 7 oz. of castor sugar, 1 oz. of Allinson cocoa, 8 eggs, the whites beaten up stiffly, 1 dessertspoonful of vanilla essence. Place the yolks of the eggs in the pan, whip them well, add the vanilla essence, the sugar, the almond meal, and the cocoa, beating the mixture all the time; add the whites of the eggs last. Pour the mixture into pie-dishes, taking care not to fill them to the top, and bake the puddings the same way as almond puddings.

CHOCOLATE MOULD.

1 quart of milk, 2 oz. of potato flour, 2 oz. of Allinson fine wheatmeal, 1 heaped-up tablespoonful of cocoa, 1 dessertspoonful of vanilla essence, and sugar to taste. Smooth the potato flour, wheatmeal flour, and cocoa with some of the milk. Add sugar to the rest of the milk, boil it up and thicken it with the smoothed ingredients. Let all simmer for 10 minutes, stir frequently, add the vanilla and mix it well through. Pour the mixture into a

wetted mould; turn out when cold, and serve plain, or with cold white sauce.

CHOCOLATE PUDDING.

1/4 lb. of grated Allinson chocolate, 1/4 lb. of flour, 1/4 lb. of sugar, 1/4 lb. of butter, 1 pint of milk, 3 eggs. Mix the chocolate, flour, sugar, and butter together. Boil up the milk and stir over the fire until it comes clean from the sides of the pan, then take it out and let it cool. Break the eggs, whisk the whites and yolks separately, first add the yolks to the pudding, and when they are well stirred in, mix in the whites. Put into a buttered basin, and steam for 1 hour. Turn out and serve hot.

CHOCOLATE PUDDING (STEAMED).

Three large sticks of chocolate, 1 pint of milk, 3 eggs, 7 oz. of Allinson fine wheatmeal, piece of vanilla 3 inches long Dissolve the chocolate in 3/4 of the pint of milk, with the rest of the milk mix the wholemeal smooth, add it to the boiled chocolate, and stir the mixture over the fire until it detaches from the sides of the saucepan; then remove it from the fire and let it cool a little. Beat up the yolks of the eggs and stir those in, whip the whites to a stiff froth and mix these well through, turn the whole into a buttered mould, and steam the pudding 1-1/2 hours. Serve with white sauce poured round.

CHOCOLATE TRIFLE.

8 sponge cakes, 3 large bars of chocolate, 1/4 pint of cream, white of 1 egg, 3 inches of stick vanilla, 3 oz. of almonds blanched and chopped, 2 oz. of ratafia, 1/2 pint of milk. Break the sponge cakes into pieces, boil the milk and pour it over them; mash them well up with a spoon. Dissolve half the chocolate in a saucepan with 2 tablespoonfuls of water, and flavour it with 1

inch of the vanilla, split; when the chocolate is quite dissolved remove the vanilla. Have ready a wetted mould, put into it a layer of sponge cake, next spread some of the dissolved chocolate, sprinkle with almonds and ratafias, repeat until you finish with a layer of sponge cake. Grate the rest of the chocolate, whip the cream with the whites of eggs, vanilla, and 1 teaspoonful of sifted sugar; sift the chocolate into the whipped cream. Turn the sponge cake mould into a glass dish, spread the chocolate cream over it evenly, and decorate it with almonds.

CHRISTMAS PUDDING (1).

1 lb. raisins (stoned), 1 lb. chopped apples, 1 lb. currants, 1 lb. breadcrumbs, 1/2 lb. mixed peel, chopped fine, 1 lb. shelled and ground Brazil nuts, 1/2 lb. chopped sweet almonds, 1 oz. bitter almonds (ground), 1 lb. sugar, 1/2 lb. butter, 1/2 oz. mixed spice, 6 eggs. Wash, pick, and dry the fruit, rub the butter into the breadcrumbs, beat up the eggs, and mix all the ingredients together; if the mixture is too dry, add a little milk. Fill some greased basins with the mixture, and boil the puddings from 8 to 12 hours.

CHRISTMAS PUDDING (2).

12 oz. breadcrumbs, 1/2 lb. currants, 1/2 lb. raisins, 1/2 lb. sweet almonds, 1 doz. bitter almonds, 3/4 lb. moist sugar, 3 oz. of butter, 2 oz. candied peel, 8 eggs, 1 teaspoonful of spice, and 1 teacupful of apple sauce. Rub the butter into the breadcrumbs, wash, pick, and dry the fruit, stone the raisins, chop or grind the almonds, beat up the eggs, mixing all well together, at the last stir in the apple sauce. Boil the pudding in a buttered mould for 8 hours, and serve with white sauce.

CHRISTMAS PUDDING (3).

1 lb. each of raisins, currants, sultanas, chopped apples, and Brazil nut kernels; 1/2 lb. each of moist sugar, wholemeal breadcrumbs, Allinson fine wheatmeal, and sweet almonds and butter; 1/4 lb. of mixed peel, 1/2 oz. of mixed spice, 6 eggs, and some milk. Wash and pick the currants and sultanas; wash and stone the raisins; chop fine the nut kernels, blanch and chop fine the almonds, and cut up fine the mixed peel. Rub the butter into the meal and breadcrumbs. First mix all the dry ingredients, then beat well the eggs and add them. Pour as much milk as is necessary to moisten the mixture sufficiently to work it with a wooden spoon. Have ready buttered pudding basins, nearly fill them with the mixture, cover with pieces of buttered paper, tie pudding cloths over the basins, and boil for 12 hours.

CHRISTMAS PUDDING (4).

This is a plainer pudding, which will agree with those who cannot take rich things. 1/2 lb. each of raisins, sultanas, currants, sugar, butter, and Brazil nuts. 1 lb. each of wholemeal breadcrumbs, Allinson fine wheatmeal, and grated carrots; 4 beaten-up eggs, 1/2 oz. of spice, and some milk. Wash and pick the currants and sultanas, wash and stone the raisins, and chop fine the Brazil nuts. Rub the butter into the wholemeal flour, mix all the ingredients together, and add as much milk as is required to moisten the mixture. Fill buttered pudding basins with it, cover with buttered paper, and tie over pudding cloths. Boil the puddings for 8 hours.

COCOA PUDDING.

1/2 lb. of stale Allinson bread, 1 pint of milk, 1 oz. of butter, 3 oz. of sifted sugar, 1 tablespoonful of Allinson cocoa, 3 eggs, vanilla to taste. Boil the bread in the milk until it is quite soft and mashed up; then add the cocoa, smoothed with a little hot water, the sugar, and vanilla. Let the mixture cool a little, add the yolks of the eggs, well beaten, then beat the whites of the eggs to a stiff froth, add these, mixing all well. Bake the pudding in a buttered dish of an hour.

COCOANUT PUDDING (1).

1/2 lb. of Allinson bread, 3 eggs, 1 pint of milk, 1 grated fresh cocoanut, its milk, and sugar to taste. Soak the bread as for the savouries, add the cocoanut, the milk of it, and sugar, and mix all well. Butter a pie-dish, pour in the mixture, place a few little pieces of butter on the top, and bake as above.

COCOANUT PUDDING (2).

10 oz. of fresh grated cocoanut, 8 oz. of Allinson breadcrumbs, 4 oz. of stoned muscatels, chopped small, 3 oz. of sugar, 3 eggs, 1 pint of milk. Mix the breadcrumbs, cocoanut; muscatels, sugar, and the butter (oiled); add the yolks of the eggs, well beaten, whip the whites of the eggs to a stiff froth, add these to the mixture just before turning the pudding into a buttered pie-dish; bake until golden brown.

COLLEGE PUDDING.

Twelve sponge fingers, 4 oz. of ratafia biscuits, 2 oz. blanched almonds, 2 oz. of candied fruit, and 1 pint of custard made with Allinson custard powder. Butter thickly a pint and a half pudding basin, decorate the bottom with a few slices of the bright coloured fruits, split the sponge fingers and arrange them round the sides of the basin, letting each one overlap the other and cut the tops level with the basin; break up the remainder of the cakes and mix with the chopped almonds, the ratafias crushed, and the remainder of the candied fruits chopped finely; carefully fill the basin with this mixture, not disturbing the fingers round the edge; prepare 1 pint of custard according to recipe on page 75, and while still hot pour into the basin over the cakes, &c., cover with a plate and put a weight on the top, let stand all night in a cold place; turn out on to a glass dish to serve.

CUSTARD PUDDING.

1 quart of milk, 2 oz. of cornflour, 2 oz. of Allinson fine wheatmeal, sugar to taste, and vanilla or other flavouring. Proceed as for a blancmange; when the ingredients are cooked, let them cool a little, beat up the eggs, and mix them well with the rest, and bake all for 20 or 30 minutes in a moderate oven.

CUSTARD PUDDING WITHOUT EGGS.

One dessertspoonful of flour, one packet of Allinson custard powder, 1 oz. of butter, 1 pint of milk, and sugar to taste. Mix the flour and custard powder to a smooth, thin paste, with a few tablespoonfuls of the milk, boil the rest of the milk with the sugar and butter; when quite boiling pour it into the powder, &c., in the basin, stir briskly, then pour into a greased pie-dish and brown slightly in the oven; before serving decorate the top with some apricot or other jam.

EMPRESS PUDDING.

1/2 lb. of rice, 2-1/2 pints of milk, the rind of 1/2 a lemon, 3 eggs, some raspberry and currant jam. Gently cook the rice with the lemon peel in the milk, until quite soft; let it cool a little and mix with it the eggs, well beaten. Butter a cake tin, place a layer of rice into it, spread a layer of jam, and repeat until the tin is full, finishing with the rice. Bake the pudding for 3/4 of an hour, turn out, and eat with boiled custard, hot or cold.

PIES

PIE-CRUSTS.

(1) 1 lb. of Allinson fine wheatmeal, 6 oz. of butter, a little cold water. Rub the butter into the meal, add enough water to the paste to keep it together, mixing it with a knife, roll out and use.

(2) 1/2 lb. of Allinson fine wheatmeal, 1/2 lb. of mashed potatoes, 3 oz. of butter, 1 tablespoonful of oil, a little cold milk (about 1 cupful). Mix the meal and mashed potatoes, rub in the butter and the oil, add enough milk to moisten the paste, mixing with a knife only, and roll out as required.

(3) 1/2 lb. of Allinson fine wheatmeal, 4 eggs, 2 oz. of butter, some milk. Rub the butter into the meal, beat the eggs well, mix them with the meal, adding enough cold milk to make a firm paste, roll out and use.

(4) 1/2 lb. of Allinson fine wheatmeal, 1/2 lb. of fine breadcrumbs, 2 eggs, 2 oz. of butter, and a little cold milk. Mix the ingredients as in (3), moisten the paste with milk, and roll it out.

(5) (Puff crust). 1 lb. of Allinson fine wheatmeal, 1 lb. of butter, a little cold water. Rub 1/2 lb. of butter into the meal, add enough cold water to make a stiff paste, roll it out, spread the paste with some of the other butter, and roll the paste up; roll it out again, spread with more butter, roll up again and repeat about 3 times, until all the butter is used up. Use for pie-crust, &c., and bake in a quick oven.

(6) 1/2 lb. of Allinson fine wheatmeal, 3 oz. of sago, 1 oz. of butter. Let the sago swell out over the fire with milk and water, mix it with the meal and butter, and roll the paste out and use.

(7) 1 lb. of Allinson fine wheatmeal, 1 gill of cold milk, 5 oz. vege-butter. Rub the butter well into the meal, moisten with the milk (taking a little

more than 1 gill if necessary), in the usual way. Roll out and use according to requirements.

TARTS

Special recipes for every kind of fruit tart are not given, as the same rules apply to all. For the crust either of the recipes given for pie-crusts may be used, and the fruit tarts can be made either open, with a bottom crust only, with top and bottom crust, or with a top crust only. When any dried fruit is used, like prunes, dried apricots, apple-rings, &c., these should first be stewed till tender, and sweetened if necessary, and allowed to cool; then place as much of the fruit as is required into your tart, cover it with a crust, and bake until the crust is done. If an open tart is made, only very little juice should be used, as it would make the crust heavy.

Summer fruit, like strawberries, raspberries, currants, cherries, and gooseberries need not be previously cooked. Mix the fruit with the necessary sugar, and it the tart is made with a top crust only, a little water can be added and an egg-cup or a little tea-cup should be placed in the pie-dish upside down to keep up the crust.

BLANCMANGE TARTLETS.

1 pint of milk, 3 oz. of ground rice, 1 teaspoonful of sugar, a few drops of almond essence, any kind of jam preferred. Make a blancmange, of the milk, ground rice, and flavouring; grease some patty pans, fill them with the blancmange mixture, place a spoonful of jam on every tartlet, and bake them 10 minutes.

CHEESECAKES (ALMOND).

3 oz. of sweet ground almonds, 1/2 oz. bitter ground almonds, 3 oz. castor sugar, 1 egg, 1 dessertspoonful of orange-water. Pound the almonds well together with the orange-water, and the sugar, beat the egg and mix it well with the almonds. Line 8 or 10 little cheesecake tins with a short crust, bake them, fill with the almond mixture, and serve cold.

CHOCOLATE TARTS.

6 oz. of Allinson fine wheatmeal, 2 oz. of butter, 2 oz. of Allinson chocolate (grated), 1 dessertspoonful of sugar, 1/2 oz. of ground rice, 4 eggs, well beaten, and 1 pint of milk. Mix the milk with the ground rice, add to it the chocolate smoothly and gradually; stir the mixture over the fire until it thickens, let cool a little and stir in the eggs; make the meal and butter into a paste with a little cold water; line a greased plate with it, and pour the cooled custard into it; bake the tart 1/2 hour in a moderate oven.

MARLBOROUGH PIE.

6 good-sized apples, 1 oz. of butter, 3 eggs, the juice and rind of 1 lemon, 1 teacupful of milk, sugar to taste, and some paste for crust. Steam or bake the apples till tender and press them through a sieve while hot, add the butter, and let the mixture cool; beat the yolks of the eggs, add to them the milk, sugar, lemon juice and rind, and add all these to the apples and butter; line a dish with paste, fill it with the above mixture, and bake the pie for 1/2 hour in a quick oven; whip the whites of the eggs stiff, adding a little castor sugar, heap the froth over the pie, and let it set in the oven.

LEMON CREAM (for Cheesecakes).

1 lb. powdered sugar, 6 yolks of eggs, 4 whites of eggs, juice of 8 lemons, grated rind of 2 lemons, 1/4 lb. fresh butter. Put the ingredients into a

double boiler and stir over a slow fire until the cream is the consistency of honey.

LEMON TART.

1 lemon, 1 breakfastcupful of water, 1 dessertspoonful of cornflour, 2 eggs, 1 oz. of butter, sugar to taste, some short crust made of 4 oz. of Allinson's fine wheatmeal and 1-1/2 oz. of butter. Moisten the cornflour with a little of the water; bring the rest of the water to the boil with the juice and the grated rind of the lemon and sugar. Thicken the mixture with the cornflour; let it simmer for a few minutes, then set aside to cool; beat up the eggs, mix them well through with the rest of the ingredients, line a flat dish or soup-plate with pastry; pour the mixture into this, cover the tart with thin strips of pastry in diamond shape, and bake the tart 3/4 of an hour.

TREACLE TART.

To 1 lb. of golden syrup add 1 breakfastcupful of Allinson breadcrumbs, the grated rind and juice of 1 lemon. Mix well together. Line the tins with short paste. Put about 1 tablespoonful of the mixture in each tin; bake in a quick oven.

BLANCMANGES

BLANCMANGE.

1 quart of milk, 2 oz. of Allinson fine wheatmeal, 2 oz. of Allinson cornflour, 1 oz. of sugar, piece of vanilla 3 inches long, or some vanilla essence. Bring 1-1/2 pints of milk to the boil, adding the vanilla spliced and the sugar; mix the wheatmeal and cornflour smooth with the rest of the milk, add the mixture to the boiling milk, stir all well for 8 to 10 minutes, and then pour it into one or two wetted moulds; when cold, turn out and serve with stewed fruit or jam.

BLANCMANGE (CHOCOLATE).

1 quart of milk, 1 oz. of N.F. cocoa, 2 oz. of Allinson cornflour, 2 oz. of sifted Allinson fine wheatmeal, sugar to taste, 1 good dessertspoonful of vanilla essence. Set the greatest part of the milk over the fire, leaving enough to smooth the cornflour, flour, and cocoa. Mix the cornflour, wheatmeal flour, and cocoa, and smooth it with the cold milk. Stir the mixture into the boiling milk, and let it all simmer for 8 to 10 minutes, stirring very frequently. Add the vanilla essence, stir it well through, pour the mixture into a wetted mould, and let it get cold. Turn it out, and serve.

BLANCMANGE (LEMON) (a very good Summer Pudding).

1 pint of water, 2 tablespoonfuls of Allinson cornflour, 1 lemon, 2 eggs, sugar to taste. Put the water in an enamel saucepan, and let it boil with the rind of the lemon in it. When boiling, add the cornflour mixed with a little

cold water. Allow it all to boil for a few minutes; then add sugar and the juice of a lemon. Have the whites of the eggs beaten to a stiff froth, and beat up well with the mixture; then pour into a mould. Make a little custard to pour over the blancmange—1/2 pint of milk, a little sugar, and essence of lemon; whisk in the yolks of the eggs. This makes an excellent custard.

BLANCMANGE EGGS.

Make a blancmange with 1 pint of milk, 1 oz. of Allinson cornflour, and 1 oz. of Allinson fine wheatmeal. Pierce the ends of 4 or 6 eggs, and let the contents drain away. Rinse the shells with cold water, then fill them with the hot blancmange mixture. When cold gently peel off the shells. Serve on a glass dish nicely arranged with stewed fruit or jam.

ORANGE MOULD (1).

7 oranges, 1 lemon, 4 oz. of cornflour, 4 oz. of sugar, 4 eggs, some water. Take the juice of the oranges and lemon and the grated rind of the latter. Add enough water to the juice to make 1 quart of liquid. Set that over the fire to boil (keeping back a 1/4 of a pint for mixing the cornflour smooth), and add the sugar. Separate the yolks of the eggs from the white; beat up the yolks and add them to the cornflour and juice when those are smooth. When the liquid over the fire boils, stir in the mixture of eggs, cornflour, and juice, and keep all stirring over the fire for 2 minutes. Have ready the whites of the eggs beaten to a stiff froth, mix it lightly with the rest, and pour the mixture into wetted moulds. Turn out when cold and serve when required.

ORANGE MOULD (2).

The juice of 7 oranges and 1 lemon, 6 oz. of sugar, 4 oz. of Allinson cornflour, and 4 eggs. Add enough water to the fruit juice to make 1 quart of liquid. Put 1-1/2 pints of this over the fire with the sugar. When boiling thicken it with the cornflour, which should be smoothed with the rest of the liquid. Stir well over the fire for 5 to 8 minutes; whip up the eggs and stir them carefully into the mixture so as not to curdle them. Pour all into a wetted mould, let it get cold, turn it out, and serve.

CREAMS

APRICOT CREAMS.

1 pint of cream, the whites of 4 eggs, some apricot jam, 2 inches of vanilla pod, 1 dessertspoonful of castor sugar. Split the vanilla, put this and the sugar into the cream; whip this with the whites of eggs until stiff, then remove the vanilla. Place a good teaspoonful of apricot jam in each custard glass, and fill up with whipped cream.

BLACKBERRY CREAM.

1 quart of blackberries, sugar to taste, 1/2 pint of cream, white of 2 eggs. Mash the fruit gently, put it into a hair-sieve and allow it to drain. Sprinkle the fruit with sugar to make the juice drain more freely; whip the cream and mix with the juice.

CHOCOLATE CREAM.

1 quart of milk, 6 oz. of Allinson chocolate, 4 eggs, 1 tablespoonful of Allinson corn flour, essence of vanilla, sugar to taste. Dissolve the chocolate in a few tablespoonfuls of water, stirring it over the fire until a thick, smooth paste; add the milk, vanilla, and sugar. When boiling thicken the milk with the cornflour; remove the mixture from the fire to cool slightly, beat the eggs well, stir them into the thickened chocolate very gradually, and stir the whole over the fire, taking care not to allow it to boil When well thickened let the cream cool; serve in custard glasses or poured over sponge cakes or macaroons.

CHOCOLATE CREAM (French) (1).

Use the whites of 3 eggs to 2 large bars of chocolate; vanilla to taste. Break the chocolate in pieces, and melt it in a little enamelled saucepan with very little water; stir it quite smooth, and flavour with Allinson vanilla essence. Set the chocolate aside until quite cold, when it should be a smooth paste, and not too firm. Beat the whites of the eggs to a very stiff froth, and mix the chocolate with it, stirring both well together until the chocolate is well mixed with the froth. It the cream is not found sweet enough, add a little castor sugar. Serve in a glass dish. This is easily made, and very dainty.

CHOCOLATE CREAM (WHIPPED).

2 oz. of Allinson chocolate to 1/4 pint of cream, white of 1 egg. Dissolve the chocolate over the fire with 2 tablespoonfuls of water; let it get quite cold, and then mix it with the cream previously whipped stiff; this will not require any additional sugar.

EGG CREAM.

The yolks of 6 eggs, 1/2 pint of water, juice of 1 lemon, 2 oz. of sifted sugar, a little cinnamon. Beat up all the ingredients, put the mixture into a saucepan over a sharp fire, and whisk it till quite frothy, taking care not to let it boil; fill into glasses and serve at once.

LEMON CREAM.

The juice of 3 lemons and the rind of 1, 7 eggs, 6 oz. of sugar, 1 dessertspoonful of cornflour. Proceed exactly as in "Orange Cream."

MACAROON CREAM.

Pound 1-1/2 doz. macaroons, place in a bowl, add 1 or 2 spoonfuls of milk, and mix all to a smooth paste. Take a 6d. jar of cream, whip to a stiff froth. Lay a little of the macaroon paste roughly in the bottom of a glass dish, then 1 or 2 spoonfuls of the cream, more paste and cream, then cover with 1 spoonful of cream put on roughly.

ORANGE CREAM.

6 oranges, 1 lemon, 7 eggs, 4 to 6 oz. of sugar (according to taste), 1 dessertspoonful of cornflour, some water. Take the juice of the oranges and the juice and grated rind of the lemon. Add enough water to the fruit juice to make 1-1/2 pints of liquid; let this get hot, adding the sugar to it; mix the cornflour smooth with a spoonful of cold water, and thicken the fruit juice with it, letting it boil up for a minute, set aside and let it cool a little; beat the eggs well, and when the liquid has cooled mix them carefully in with it; return the whole over a gentle fire, keep stirring continually until the cream thickens, but take care not to let it boil, as this would curdle it. When cold, serve in custard glasses, or in a glass dish poured over macaroons.

RASPBERRY CREAM.

1 quart of raspberries, sugar to taste, 1/2 pint of cream. Proceed as in "Blackberry Cream."

RUSSIAN CREAM.

Lay 6 sponge cakes on a glass dish, and soak them with any fruit syrup; then add 1 pint of blancmange. When nearly cold cover the top with ratafia biscuits and decorate with angelica and cherries.

STRAWBERRY CREAM.

1 quart of strawberries, sugar to taste, 1/2 pint of cream. Proceed as in "Blackberry Cream."

SWISS CREAM.

1/2 pint of cream, 1/2 pint of milk, 1 tablespoonful of Allinson cornflour, 1/4 lb. of macaroons, 2 oz. of ratafias, vanilla, and sugar to taste. Put the cream and milk over the fire, adding a piece of vanilla 2 inches long, and sugar to taste; smooth the cornflour with a tablespoonful of cold milk, mix it with the milk and cream when nearly boiling, stir the mixture over the fire until it has thickened and let it simmer 2 minutes longer, always stirring; remove the vanilla, arrange the macaroons and ratafias on a shallow glass dish, let the cream cool a little, then pour it over the biscuits and serve cold. This makes a delicious dish.

WHIPPED CREAMS.

Quantity of good thick cream according to requirement. The white of 1 egg to 1/4 pint. Whip it well with a whisk or fork until it gets quite thick; in hot weather it should be kept on ice or standing in another basin with cold water, as the cream might curdle. Add sugar to taste and whatever flavouring might be desired, this latter giving the cream its name. When whipped cream is used to pour over sweets, &c., flavour it with stick vanilla; a piece 1 inch long is sufficient for 1/2 pint of cream; it must be split and as much as possible of the little grains in it rubbed into the cream.

CUSTARDS

ALMOND CUSTARD.

1 quart of milk, 6 eggs, 1 dessertspoonful of Allinson cornflour, 1 wineglassful of rosewater, sugar to taste, 1/2 lb. ground almonds. Boil the milk with the sugar and almonds; smooth the cornflour with the rosewater and stir it into the boiling milk, let it boil up for a minute. Beat up the eggs, leaving out 3 of the whites of the eggs, which are to be beaten to a stiff froth. Let the milk cool a little, then stir in the eggs very gradually, taking care not to curdle them; stir over the fire until the custard is nearly boiling, then let it cool, stirring occasionally; pour it into a glass dish, and pile the whipped whites of the eggs on the top of the custard just before serving.

BAKED APPLE CUSTARD.

8 large apples, moist sugar to taste, half a teacupful of water and the juice of half a lemon, 1 pint of custard made with Allinson custard powder. Peel, cut and core the apples and put into a lined saucepan with the water, sugar, and lemon juice, stew till tender and rub through a sieve; when cold put the fruit at the bottom of a pie-dish and pour the custard over, grate a little nutmeg over the top, bake lightly, and serve cold.

BAKED CUSTARD.

1 quart of milk, 6 eggs, sugar, and flavouring to taste. Heat the milk until nearly boiling, sweeten it with sugar, and add any kind of flavouring. Whip up the eggs, and mix them carefully with the hot milk. Pour the custard into

a buttered pie-dish, and bake it in a moderately hot oven until set. If the milk and eggs are mixed cold and then baked the custard goes watery; it is therefore important to bear in mind that the milk should first be heated. Serve with stewed fruit.

CARAMEL CUSTARD.

1-1/2 pints of milk, 4 eggs, 1 dessertspoonful of sugar, 1/2 lemon and 4 oz. of castor sugar for caramel. Put the dry castor sugar into an enamelled saucepan and let it melt and turn a rich brown over the fire, stirring all the time. When the sugar is melted and browned stir into it about 2 tablespoonfuls of hot water, and the juice of 1/2 lemon. Then pour the caramel into a mould or cake-tin, and let it run all round the sides of the tin. Meanwhile heat the milk near boiling-point, and add the vanilla and sugar. Whip up the eggs, stir carefully into them the hot milk, so as not to curdle the eggs. Then pour the custard into the tin on the caramel and stand the tin in a larger tin with hot water, place it in the oven, and bake in a moderately hot oven for about 20 minutes or until the custard is set. Allow it to get cold, turn out, and serve.

CARAMEL CUP CUSTARD (French).

Make the custard as in the recipe for "Cup Custard." Take 4 oz. of castor sugar; put it over a brisk fire in a small enamelled saucepan, keep stirring it until quite melted and a rich brown. Then cautiously add 2 tablespoonfuls of boiling water, taking care not to be scalded by the spluttering sugar. Gradually stir the caramel into the hot custard. Let it cool, and serve in custard glasses.

CUP CUSTARD.

6 whole eggs or 10 yolks of eggs, 1 quart of milk, sugar and vanilla to taste. Beat the eggs well while the milk is being heated. Use vanilla pods to flavour—they are better than the essence, which is alcoholic; split a piece of the pod 3 or 4 inches long, and let it soak in the milk for 1 hour before it is set over the fire, so as to extract the flavour from the vanilla. Sweeten the milk and let it come nearly to boiling-point. Carefully stir the milk into the beaten eggs, adding only a little at a time, so as not to curdle the eggs. When all is mixed, pour the custard into a jug, which should be placed in a saucepanful of boiling water. Keep stirring the custard with a wooden spoon, and as soon as the custard begins to coat the spoon remove the saucepan from the fire, and continue stirring the custard until it is well thickened. In doing as here directed there is no risk of the custard curdling, for directly the water ceases to boil it cannot curdle the custard, although it is hot enough to finish thickening it. If the milk is nearly boiling when mixed with the eggs, the custard will only take from 5 to 10 minutes to finish. When the custard is done place the jug in which it was made in a bowl of cold water, stir it often while cooling to prevent a skin forming on the top. Remove the vanilla pod and pour the custard into glasses. Should the custard be required very thick, 8 eggs should be used, or the milk can first be thickened with a dessertspoonful of Allinson cornflour before mixing it with the 6 eggs. This is an excellent plan; it saves eggs, and the custard tastes just as rich as if more eggs were used. Serve in custard glasses, or in a glass dish.

CUSTARD (ALLINSON).

1 pint of milk or cream, 2 oz. of lump sugar and 1 packet of Allinson custard powder. Put the contents of the packet into a basin and mix to a smooth, thin paste with about 2 tablespoonfuls of the milk; boil the remainder of milk with the sugar, and when quite boiling pour quickly into the basin, stirring thoroughly; stir occasionally until quite cold, then pour into custard glasses and grate a little nutmeg on the top, or put in a glass dish and serve with stewed or tinned fruits, or the custard can be used with Christmas or plum pudding instead of sauce.

When the custard has been standing over night, it should be well stirred before using.

CUSTARD IN PASTRY OR KENTISH PUDDING PIE.

Line a pie-dish with puff paste, prick well with a fork and bake carefully, then fill the case with a custard made as follows. Mix 1 dessertspoonful of flour with the contents of a packet of Allinson custard powder, out of a pint of milk take 8 tablespoonfuls and mix well with the flour, custard powder, &c., boil the remainder of milk with sugar to taste and 1 oz. of butter and when quite boiling pour on to the custard powder, stir quickly for a minute, then pour into the pastry case, grate a little nutmeg on the top and bake till of a golden brown; serve either hot or cold.

FRUMENTY.

1 quart of milk, 1/2 pint of ready boiled wheat (boiled in water), 1/4 lb. of sultanas and currants mixed, sugar to taste, 4 eggs, a stick of cinnamon. Mix the milk with the wheat (which should be fresh), the sugar and fruit, adding the cinnamon, and let all cook gently over a low fire, stirring frequently; when the mixture is nicely thickened remove it from the fire and let it cool; beat up the eggs and gradually mix them with the rest, taking great care not to curdle them. Stir the frumenty over the fire, but do not allow to boil. Serve hot or cold. The wheat should be fresh and soaked for 24 hours, and then cooked from 3 to 5 hours.

GOOSEBERRY CUSTARD.

Make some good puff paste and line a pie-dish with it, putting a double row round the edge. With 1/2 lb. of castor sugar stew 1 lb. of green gooseberries until the skins are tender, then rub them through a sieve. Scald 1 pint of milk, mix 1 tablespoonful of Allinson cornflour to a smooth paste with cold milk, add it to the milk when boiling, let it boil for 5 minutes, gently stirring it all the time, then turn it into a bowl and let it become cool. Add 1/4 lb. of castor sugar, 2 oz. of butter melted and dropped in gradually whilst the mixture is beaten, then put in the well-beaten yolks of 6 eggs, add the mashed gooseberries in small quantities, and lastly the whites of the eggs whipped to a stiff froth; beat all together for a minute to mix well. Pour this into the lined pie-dish and bake 25 or 30 minutes; serve in the pie-dish. This can be made from any kind of acid fruit, and is as good cold as hot.

GOOSEBERRY FOOL.

Top and tail 1 pint of gooseberries, put into a lined saucepan with sugar to taste and half a small teacupful of water, stew gently until perfectly tender, rub through a sieve, and when quite cold add 1 pint of custard made with Allinson custard powder, which should have been allowed to become cold before being mixed with the fruit. Serve in a glass dish with sponge fingers.

N.B.—Apple fool is made in exactly the same way as above, substituting sharp apples for the gooseberries.

MACARONI CUSTARD.

4 oz. of Allinson macaroni, 3 eggs, 1 tablespoonful of sugar, 1 even dessertspoonful of Allinson cornflour, vanilla to taste. Boil the macaroni in 1 pint of milk, and add a little water it needed; when quite tender place it on a glass dish to cool; make a custard of the rest of the milk and the other ingredients; flavour it well with vanilla; when the custard is cool pour it over the macaroni, and serve with or without stewed fruit.

MACAROON CUSTARD.

1/2 lb. of macaroons, 1 quart of milk, 6 eggs, 1 dessertspoonful of Allinson cornflour, sugar and vanilla essence to taste. Boil the milk and stir into it the cornflour smoothed with a little of the milk; whip up the eggs, and carefully stir in the milk (which should have been allowed to go off the boil) without curdling it; add sugar and vanilla to taste, and stir the custard over the fire until it thickens, placing it in a jug into a saucepan of boiling water. Arrange the macaroons in a glass dish, and when the custard is cool enough not to crack the dish, pour it over them and sprinkle some ground almonds on the top. Serve cold.

ORANGE CUSTARD.

The juice of 6 oranges and of 1/2 a lemon, 6 eggs, 6 oz. of sugar, and 1 dessertspoonful of Allinson cornflour. Add enough water to the fruit juices to make 1-1/2 pints of liquid. Set this over the fire with the sugar; meanwhile smooth the cornflour with a little cold water, and thicken the liquid with it when boiling. Set aside the saucepan, (which should be an enamelled one) so as to cool the contents a little. Beat up the eggs, gradually stir into them the thickened liquid, and then proceed with the custard as in the previous recipe. This is a German sweet, and very delicious.

RASPBERRY CUSTARD.

1-1/2 pints of raspberries, 1/2 pint of red currants, 6 oz. of sugar, 7 eggs, 1 dessertspoonful of Allinson cornflour. Mix the fruit, and let it cook from 5 to 10 minutes with 1 pint of water; strain the juice well through a piece of muslin or a fine hair-sieve. There should be 1 quart of juice; if necessary add a little more water; return the juice to the saucepan, add the sugar and reheat the liquid; when it boils thicken it with the cornflour, then set it aside to cool. Beat up the eggs, add them carefully after the fruit juice has somewhat cooled; stir the custard over the fire until it thickens, but do not allow it to boil, as the eggs would curdle. Serve cold in custard glasses, or in a glass dish poured over macaroons or sponge cakes. You can make a fruit custard in this way, with strawberries, cherries, red currants, or any juicy summer fruit.

STRAWBERRY CUSTARD.

Remove the stalks from 1 lb. of fresh strawberries, place them in a glass dish and scatter over 2 tablespoonfuls of pounded sugar; prepare 1 pint of custard with Allinson custard powder according to recipe given above, and while still hot pour carefully over the fruit, set aside to cool, and just before serving (which must not be until the custard has become quite cold) garnish the top with a few fine strawberries.

APPLE COOKERY

APPLES (BUTTERED).

1 lb. of apples, 2 oz. of butter, ground cinnamon and sugar to taste. Pare, core, and slice the apples; heat the butter in a frying-pan, when it boils turn in the apples and fry them until cooked; sprinkle with sugar and cinnamon, and serve on buttered toast.

APPLE CAKE

6 oz. each of Allinson fine wheatmeal and white flour, 4-1/2 oz. of butter, 1 egg, a little cold water, 1-1/2 lbs. of apples, 1 heaped-up teaspoonful of cinnamon, and 3 oz. of castor sugar. Rub the butter into the meal and flour, beat up the egg and add it, and as much cold water as is required to make a smooth paste; roll out the greater part of it 1/4 inch thick, and line a flat buttered tin with it. Pare, core, and cut the apples into thin divisions, arrange them in close rows on the paste point down, leaving 1 inch of edge uncovered; sift the sugar and cinnamon over the apples; roll out thinly the rest of the paste, cover the apples with it, turn up the edges of the bottom crust over the edges of the top crust, make 2 incisions in the crust, and bake the cake until brown in a moderately hot oven; when cold sift castor sugar over it, slip the cake off the tin, cut into pieces, and serve.

APPLE CHARLOTTE.

2 lbs. of good cooking apples, 2 oz. of chopped almonds, 4 oz. of currants and sultanas mixed, 1 stick of cinnamon about 3 inches long, sugar to taste,

the juice of 1/2 a lemon, and Allinson bread and butter cut very thinly. Pare, core, and cut up the apples, and stew them with a teacupful of water and the cinnamon, until the apples have become a pulp; remove the cinnamon, and add sugar, lemon juice, the almonds, and the currants and sultanas, previously picked, washed, and dried; mix all well and allow the mixture to cool; butter a pie-dish and line it with thin slices of bread and butter, then place on it a layer of apple mixture, repeat the layers, finishing with slices of bread and butter; bake for 3/4 hour in a moderate oven.

APPLES (DRYING).

Those who have apple-trees are often at a loss to know what to do with the windfalls. The apples come down on some days by the bushel, and it is impossible to use them all up for apple pie, puddings, or jelly. An excellent way to keep them for winter use is to dry them. It gives a little trouble, but one is well repaid for it, for the home-dried apples are superior in flavour to any bought apple-rings or pippins. Peel your apples, cut away the cores and all the worm-eaten parts—for nearly the whole of the windfalls are more or less worm-eaten. The good parts cut into thin pieces, spread them on large sheets of paper in the sun. In the evening (before the dew falls), they should be taken indoors and spread on tins (but with paper underneath), on the cool kitchen stove, and if the oven is only just warm, placed in the oven well spread out; of course they require frequent turning about, both in the sun and on the stove. Next day they may again be spread in the sun, and will probably be quite dry in the course of the day. Should the weather be rainy, the apples must be dried indoors only, and extra care must then be taken that they are neither scorched nor cooked on the stove. Whilst cooking is going on they will dry nicely on sheets of paper on the plate-rack. When the apples are quite dry, which is when the outside is not moist at all, fill them into brown paper bags and hang them up in an airy, dry place. The apples will be found delicious in flavour when stewed, and most acceptable when fresh fruit is scarce. I have dried several bushels of apples in this way every year.

APPLE DUMPLINGS.

Core as many apples as may be required. Fill the holes with a mixture of sugar and cinnamon; make a paste for a short crust, roll it out, and wrap each apple in it. Bake the dumplings about 30 or 40 minutes in the oven, or boil them the same time in plenty of water, placing the dumplings in the water when it boils fast. Serve with cream or sweet white sauce.

APPLE FOOL.

2 lbs. of apples, 1/2 lb. of dates, 3/4 pint of milk, 1/4 pint of cream, 6 cloves tied in muslin, and a little sugar. Pare, core, and cut up the apples, stone the dates, and gently stew the fruit with a teacupful of water and the cloves until quite tender; when sufficiently cooked, remove the cloves, and rub the fruit through a sieve; gradually mix in the milk, which should be boiling, then the cream; serve cold with sponge-cake fingers.

APPLE FRITTERS.

3 good juicy cooking apples, 3 eggs, 6 oz. of Allinson fine wheatmeal, 1/2 pint of milk, and sugar to taste. Pare and core the apples, and cut them into rounds 1/4 inch thick; make a batter with the milk, meal, and the eggs well beaten, adding sugar to taste. Have a frying-pan ready on the fire with boiling oil, vege-butter, or butter, dip the apple slices into the batter and fry the fritters until golden brown; drain them on blotting paper, and keep them hot in the oven until all are done.

APPLE JELLY.

1 pint of water to each 1 lb. of apples. Wash and cut up the apples, and boil them in the water until tender; then pour them into a jelly bag and let drain

well; take 1 lb. of loaf sugar to each pint of juice, and the juice of 1 lemon to each quart of liquid. Boil the liquid, skimming carefully, until the jelly sets when cold if a drop is tried on a plate. It may take from 2 hours to 3 hours in boiling.

APPLE PANCAKES.

Make the batter as directed in the recipe for "Apple Fritters," peel 2 apples, and cut them in thin slices, mix them with the batter, add sugar and cinnamon to taste, a little lemon juice if liked, and fry the pancakes in the usual way.

APPLE PUDDING.

1-1/2 lbs. of apples, 1 teaspoonful of ground cinnamon, sugar to taste, 1/2 lb. of Allinson fine wheatmeal, and 2-1/2 oz. of butter or vege-butter. Pare, core, and cut up the apples; make a paste of the meal, butter and a little cold water; roll the paste out, line a pudding basin with the greater part of it, put in the apples, and sprinkle over them the cinnamon and 4 oz. of sugar—a little more should the apples be very sour; cover the apples with the rest of the paste, and press the edges together round the sides; tie a cloth over the basin and boil the pudding for 2-1/2 to 3 hours in a saucepan with boiling water.

APPLE PUDDING (Nottingham).

6 baking apples, 2 oz. of sugar, 1 heaped up teaspoonful of ground cinnamon, 3/4 pint of milk, 3 eggs, 6 oz. of Allinson wholemeal, and 1 oz. of butter. Core the apples, mix the sugar and cinnamon, and fill the hole where the core was with it; put the apples into a buttered pie-dish; make a batter of the milk, eggs, and meal, melt the butter and mix it into the batter;

pour it over the apples, and bake the pudding for 2 hours in a moderate oven.

APPLE SAGO.

5 oz. of sago, 1-1/2 lbs. of apples, the juice of a lemon, a teaspoonful of ground cinnamon, and sugar to taste. Wash the sago and cook it in 1-1/2 pints of water, to which the cinnamon is added; meanwhile have the apples ready, pared, cored, and cut up; cook them in very little water, just enough to keep the apples from burning; when they are quite soft rub them through a sieve and mix them with the cooking sago, adding sugar and lemon juice; let all cook gently for a few minutes or until the sago is quite soft; put the mixture into a wetted mould, and turn out when cold.

APPLE SAUCE.

1 lb. of good cooking apples, sugar to taste. Pare, core, and cut in pieces the apples, cook them in a few spoonfuls of water to prevent them burning; when quite soft rub the apple through a sieve, and sweeten the sauce to taste. Rubbing the sauce through a sieve ensures the sauce being free from pieces should the apple not pulp evenly.

APPLE TART (OPEN).

2 lbs. of apples, 1 cupful of currants and sultanas, 2 oz. of chopped almonds, sugar to taste, 1 teaspoonful of ground cinnamon or the rind of 1/2 lemon (which latter should be removed after cooking with the apples), 12 oz. or Allinson fine wheatmeal, and 4-1/2 oz. of butter. Pare, core, and cut up the apples; stew them in very little water, only just enough to keep from burning; when nearly done add the currants, sultanas, almonds, cinnamon, and sugar; let all simmer together until the apples have become a pulp; let

the fruit cool; make a paste of the meal, butter, and a little water; roll it out and line a round, flat dish with it, and brush the paste over with white of eggs; turn the apple mixture on the paste; cut the rest of the paste into strips 3/8 of an inch wide, and lay them over the apples in diamond shape, each 1 inch from the other, so as to make a kind of trellis arrangement of the pastry. If enough paste is left, lay a thin strip right round the dish to finish off the edge, mark it nicely with a fork or spoon, and bake the tart for 3/4 hour. Serve with white sauce or custard.

APPLES (RICE)

2 lbs. of apples, 1/2 lb. of rice, the rind of 1/2 lemon (or a piece of stick cinnamon if preferred), 4 oz. of sultanas, sugar to taste, 1 oz. of butter, and, if the apples are not sour, the juice of a lemon. Boil the rice in 3 pints of water with the lemon rind, then add the apples, pared, cored, and sliced, the sultanas, butter, lemon juice, and sugar; let all simmer gently for 1/2 hour, or until quite tender; if too dry add a little more water; remove the lemon rind before serving.

EVE PUDDING.

1/2 lb. each of apples and breadcrumbs, and 1/2 lb. of currants and sultanas mixed, 5 eggs well beaten, sugar to taste, the grated rind and juice of 1 lemon, and 2 oz. of butter. Peel, core, and chop small the apples, mix them with the breadcrumbs, sugar, currants, and sultanas (washed and picked), the lemon juice and rind, and the butter, previously melted; whip up the eggs and mix them well with the other ingredients; turn the mixture into a buttered mould, tie with a cloth, and steam the pudding for 3 hours.

BREAD AND CAKES

THE ADVANTAGES OF WHOLEMEAL BREAD.

People are now concerning themselves about the foods they eat, and inquiring into their properties, composition, and suitability. One food that is now receiving a good deal of attention is bread, and we ought to be sure that this is of the best kind, for as a nation we eat daily a pound of it per head. We consume more of this article of food than of any other, and this is as it ought to be, for bread is the staff of life, and many of the other things we eat are garnishings. It is said we cannot live on bread alone, but this is untrue if the loaf is a proper one; at one time our prisoners were fed on it alone, and the peasantry of many countries live on very little else.

Not many years ago books treating of food and nutrition always gave milk as the standard food, and so it is for calves and babies. Nowadays we use a grain food as the standard, and of all grains wheat is the one which is nearest perfection, or which supplies to the body those elements that it requires, and in best proportions. A perfect food must contain carbonaceous, nitrogenous, and mineral matter in definite quantities; there must be from four to six parts of carbonaceous or heat and force-forming matter to one of nitrogen, and from two to four per cent. of mineral matter; also a certain bulk of innutritious matter for exciting secretion, for separating the particles of food so that the various gastric and intestinal juices may penetrate and dissolve out all the nutriment, and for carrying off the excess of the biliary and other intestinal secretions with the fæces.

A grain of wheat consists of an outer hard covering or skin, a layer of nitrogenous matter directly under this, and an inner kernel of almost pure starch. The average composition of wheat is this:—

```
            Nitrogen         12
            Carbon           72
            Mineral Matter    4
            Water            12
```

From this analysis we observe that the nitrogenous matter is to the carbonaceous in the proportion of one-sixth, which is the composition of a perfect food. Besides taking part in this composition, the bran, being in a great measure insoluble, passes in bulk through the bowels, assisting daily laxation—a most important consideration. If wheat is such a perfect food, it must follow that wholemeal bread must be best for our daily use. That such is the case, evidence on every side shows; those who eat it are healthier, stronger, and more cheerful than those who do not, all other things being equal. Wholemeal bread comes nearer the standard of a perfect food than does the wheaten grain, as in fermentation some of the starch is destroyed, and thus the proportion of nitrogen is slightly increased.

The next question is, how shall we prepare the grain so as to make the best bread from it? This is done by grinding the grain as finely as possible with stones, and then using the resulting flour for bread-making. The grain should be first cleaned and brushed, and passed over a magnet to cleanse it from any bits of steel or iron it may have acquired from the various processes it goes through, and then finely ground. To ensure fine grinding, it is always advisable to kiln-dry it first. When ground, nothing must be taken from it, nor must anything be added to the flour, and from this bread should be made. Baking powder, soda, and tartaric acid, or soda and hydrochloric acid, or ammonia and hydrochloric acid, or other chemical agents, must never be used for raising bread, as these substances are injurious, and affect the human system for harm. The only ferment that should be used is yeast; of this the French variety is best. If brewer's yeast is used it must be first well washed, otherwise it gives a bitter flavour to the loaf. A small quantity of salt may be used, but not much, otherwise it adds an injurious agent to the bread.

www.ingramcontent.com/pod-product-compliance
Lightning Source LLC
Chambersburg PA
CBHW081121080526
44587CB00021B/3692